Selling Leverage:
How to Motivate People to Buy

SELLING LEVERAGE:
How to Motivate
People to Buy

William Exton, Jr.

Prentice-Hall, Inc.   Englewood Cliffs, New Jersey

Prentice-Hall International, Inc., *London*
Prentice-Hall of Australia, Pty. Ltd., *Sydney*
Prentice-Hall Canada Inc., *Toronto*
Prentice-Hall of India Private Ltd., *New Delhi*
Prentice-Hall of Japan, Inc., *Tokyo*
Prentice-Hall of Southeast Asia Pte. Ltd., *Singapore*
Whitehall Books, Ltd., *Wellington, New Zealand*
Editora Prentice-Hall do Brasil Ltda., *Rio de Janeiro*

© 1984 by

William Exton, Jr.

Library of Congress Cataloging in Publication Data

Exton, William.
  Selling leverage.

  Includes index.
  1. Selling—Psychological aspects.   I. Title.
HF5438.8.P75E93   1984   658.8'5   83-22948
ISBN 0-13-805433-9
ISBN 0-13-805425-8 {PBK}

Printed in the United States of America

In Memory of
MANNING MASON PHILLIPS EXTON
1908–1978

Exemplary in many roles: husband, father, son, business executive, naval officer, scholar, civil servant, artist, connoisseur of
culture, sportsman, and—longest of all—for seventy years, my
brother; companion of my youth and—in many ways—a
challenging model of so many admirable traits, which could be
found only in such a notable character as his.

How This Book
Will Help You
Sell Successfully
in Today's Tough
Business Climate

You know that there is never a sale without the *motivation* to buy; the prospect becomes a customer only when *motivated* to make the buying decision. This book tells, for the first time, how to motivate the prospect by selling with the decisive advantages of leverage. It tells how you can command this persuasive power to motivate the prospect by using the basic principle of Motivational Selling Leverage—a principle that can make the decisive difference in your selling.

That simple but enormously effective device, the lever, long ago revolutionized mechanics and engineering. Other applications of that same principle of leverage also made possible many of our important advances in science, technology, investment, finance, and management. Now it can also bring that same kind of tremendous advantage to you, by helping you to multiply the motivational power of your selling.

There are three basic components of motivation, just as there are three basic elements in leverage. In selling, the three basic components of leverage parallel the three basic components of motivation. That parallel between motivation and leverage makes Motivational Selling Leverage the natural and therefore the most effective way to sell.

As a successsful salesperson it is you who must make more and bigger sales—by knowing the best way to *motivate* your prospects to purchase. This book helps you do just that. Look over the list of contents. It shows how this book will help you sell more successfully by providing you with a workable understanding of motivation and a blueprint for applying the primary elements of motivation to make the principles of selling work better for you.

Selling Leverage, therefore, provides a new and advanced kind of guidance to help you:

- Bring about the Three Motivational Requirements for the prospect to say "Yes." You will learn how the common lever serves as a useful, clarifying analogy to the process of selling. (See Chapter 1.)

- Make specific plans to develop the best combination of the Three Primary Elements of Leverage for each sale. (See Chapter 2.)

- Relate this analysis to your own individuality to bring about the most favorable relationship for making the sale. (See Chapter 3.)

- Determine the practical objective for each prospective sale. (See Chapter 4.)

- Analyze the prospect, so that you know what benefits will have the greatest motivational appeal. (See Chapter 5.)

- Start with and develop the right selling relationship, the right opening, and the right first impression. (See Chapter 6.)

- Apply your selling communication most effectively to present the benefits in the best way to secure your objective; and utilize the relationship you have built to increase your Motivational Selling Leverage. How to use the right facts at the right time. (See Chapter 7.)

- Overcome hidden traps in sales resistance, competition, and closing. New techniques for recognizing, analyzing, and overcoming problems and obstacles. (See Chapter 8.)

By helping you to do all these things well, Selling Leverage can help you to sell successfully.

Long ago a very wise man named Archimedes said: "Give me a lever long enough, and a fulcrum, and I will move the world!" He meant that whatever the difficulty, you can still produce the results you want *if* you apply the right Leverage!

When you want to move something, and therefore need to make the most of whatever strength or ability you have, your best bet, of course, is to use a *Lever*. That very important bit of basic engineering know-how also applies to *selling*.

Now, anyone who really wants to sell can also develop that same positive "can do," confident attitude—just like Archimedes!—about approaching *any* prospect; and know that he/she can do a truly professional job of selling by using Motivational Selling Leverage.

Selling Leverage actually improves on Archimedes! It provides a complete, total system for motivating the prospect to buy. And, of course, this helps you to produce the best possible sales results.

Selling Leverage helps you apply the soundest and most effective combination of the basic principles of selling to motivate the prospect to buy, to build the strongest selling arguments, and to make the very most of your own ability to sell.

What is the mark of the professional salesperson? What makes him or her effective and successful? The professionals *know* what they are doing and *why*. They are well prepared. They are aware of what they need to know to make the sale and they know how to find this out.

You, the sales professional, are confident, because you know the odds are with you.

To put it in terms of golf, I am talking about salespersons who are like the real, tournament-winning "pro"—the player who carefully examines the lie of the ball, who knows just where the ball should go, what kind of stroke to make, what club to use, how to make the stroke, and who then makes the stroke, with very much the intended results.

I am not talking about "amateurs"—whatever their handicap—who think wishfully about how far and where they would like the ball to go; or timidly, about where they dare try to go; and who then play with inadequate confidence, unpredictable tee technique, and great reliance on luck.

This book can help you to be a "pro," or a better "pro." It can help you understand the critical factors affecting each prospect and each selling situation. It can help you judge the best way to handle the prospect and the situation, and to go on from there to make the sale.

Not only can this book help you to understand the prospect and the situation, but it can also help you to understand yourself better, and therefore to "manage" better the only real selling "tool" you have—*yourself*.

If you understand the prospect and the selling situation well enough, and know what to do, you can often turn the prospect, or the selling situation—or both—into selling assets; almost as if they were tools to help you build and shape the sale. This is the highest goal of the truly professional salesperson; and it is the true objective of Motivational Selling Leverage.

This book is planned systematically to help you create for yourself your own personal system of selling—the most effective system of selling that can be developed by you with your existing personality, knowledge and experience, for application to the products or services you want to sell, in the markets where you expect to operate, and to the prospects you will have to satisfy.

The book follows a sequence of concepts. If you follow this sequence carefully, you will learn about Motivational Selling Leverage and how to apply its basic principles in all your selling contacts. You will learn about natural selling and how to use it to develop motivation to buy.

With Selling Leverage you will not only sell better, but you will also enjoy selling a great deal more.

William Exton, Jr.

Table of Contents

Selling Leverage: Scientific Sales Tool That Wins Prospects and Makes Them Want to Buy

The Enormous Power of Motivation

If you want to influence or affect what others do, you must have some understanding of the workings of human motivation—that force within us so powerful that it really decides what we do (or don't do)—how we do it— and why.

The world is full of striking examples of the extraordinary power of motivation. Every war or revolution gives us thousands of examples of men and women so motivated by patriotism or ideology to gain victory for their own side that they not only risk their lives, but in some cases willingly sacrifice them to help their side win. Thousands more have been so motivated by loyalty to their religions, ideas, or causes that they have refused to give them up, even under the most terrible sufferings, imprisonment, and torture.

Think of the thousands of penniless immigrants who could not speak the language when they came, who were so motivated to be successful in their new homeland that they managed to overcome all obstacles, and even managed, sometimes, to become wealthy and famous.

Scientists have been motivated to pursue "far-out" theories, shared by few or none of their colleagues, until they succeeded in proving the validity of their ideas.

1

Parents have been motivated to make many sacrifices to educate their children.

Lovers have been motivated to endure severe frustrations in the hope of eventual union.

Artists and writers have been so motivated to concentrate on their creative goals that they have lived in privation for years while striving for recognition.

Many outstanding politicians have been motivated to continue to seek support when, at first, few would listen to them.

Thousands of people who now own their own businesses or control their own companies began their careers with little besides their ambition and the motivation to succeed.

Motivation is the "why" behind everything we do. Without motivation we would do nothing!

If the potential is there, motivation can change a limp, motionless body into an active, skillful, triumphant athlete or a fabulous dancer. Motivation turns ordinary people into marathon runners, daredevil stuntmen, deep sea divers, steeplejacks, parachute jumpers, and explorers. Motivation sends people soaring in hang gliders, or scaling mountain peaks "just because they are there."

If you really want to be a success in selling, you need to understand motivation. You also need to apply it effectively and adaptively to each selling situation. That's the whole idea behind Motivational Selling Leverage.

The Tremendous Importance of Motivation

Everything we do, we do because of motivation. Motivation works on all of us, in very ordinary ways, all the time. Motivation gets us out of bed in the morning (eagerly or reluctantly), and to the breakfast table, and to work, and so on, throughout the day. Everything we do, we do because we are motivated to do it—whether we do it well or badly, willingly or unwillingly; and whether we enjoy it or not.

If our motivations come from within us—if they arise from values that are truly meaningful—then they are positive, and can propel us to achievements we never knew we could accomplish.

Sometimes our motivations are negative; they move us to avoid some foreseen consequence or penalty. Such motivations are usually forced upon us. (If I don't get up now, I'll be late, and I'll get a call-down. If I don't get this job done, I may be fired. If I don't make my quota, I'll be in trouble.) Such motivations may be strong enough for us to avoid whatever we want to avoid, but they are usually not positive enough to power all that we can or should do.

Motivational Selling Leverage can provide powerful positive motivation to make you want to sell more and better. It can also help you to develop positive motivation in your prospects and customers to make them want to buy—and to buy from you.

Why Motivation Is Indispensable to Selling

Why do people buy anything? They need it, want it, or just "feel like buying it"—for one reason or other. They may be acting out of desperation, necessity, careful market study, impulse, or whim. Each situation involves a different kind of motivation—but motivation has to be there—or there'll be no sale.

Yes, motivation is indispensable to selling, and motivation is the basic factor in every sale. But the prospect must have that motivation to buy before you can make the sale. If you have enough motivation to do the selling, and if you back it up with the right know-how, you can create that motivation in the prospect.

It is all really very simple if you think of it this way. You may be lucky enough to be the only one who is selling something everybody wants; or you may be able to sell at a price nobody else can beat; or you may happen to know, or run into, enough prospects who already have enough motivation to buy from you. In any such situation, you don't have to sell. All you have to do is take orders.

If you are not that lucky; and if you really do want to—or need to—do more than just take orders from people who don't need to be sold—then you will have to do something to motivate people (or to strengthen their motivation) to buy—and to buy what *you* are selling; and to buy it from *you*.

And that is what this book is all about.

The Power That Makes the Difference Between "Yes" and "No"

Let us begin by looking at the two extremes that salespeople encounter: "no" and "yes." Doing this can help you to understand better the really important situations between such extremes.

There is such a thing, of course, as an absolutely, positively unchangeable "no." This reflects not only a lack of motivation to buy, but also a strong, *negative* motivation, influenced by reasons *not* to buy. There is also such a thing as an unquestionably determined "yes," which, of course, reflects *positive* motivation that is based on reasons for buying.

Well, anybody can walk away from that hopeless "no"; and anybody can sign up that eager "yes." But both of these extremes are rare. Practically every sales situation is somewhere between these two extremes; and if it isn't a final "yes" or "no," we can label it a "maybe." In every "maybe" situation, there are motivations in both directions: motivations based on reasons to buy, and motivations based on reasons not to buy. Therefore, you have a chance to turn almost every "maybe" into a "yes!" To do this you have to bring about enough of a change in the prospect's motivations to create a motivational balance that is *favorable to you.* And you do it by working on those reasons, until the reasons to buy outweigh the reasons not to buy, and the positive motivations outweigh the negative motivations.

In every "maybe" situation, the reasons not to buy can become less motivating, and the reasons to buy can become more motivating. Then the motivational balance becomes more favorable, and your prospect is motivated to say "yes."

So you see that motivation is the power that makes the difference between "yes" and "no." And *that power* is what Motivational Selling Leverage is all about.

The motivations which work for you or against you in trying to make a sale are all "inside the prospect"; and *that* is what you have to work on. So you have to recognize the prospect's motivations and understand them. The prospect "has reasons" for these motivations, and you can find out what those reasons are. You can figure out which of the prospect's reasons, for or against the sale, are the most motivating and why. Then you can work to overcome the negative reasons, while you strengthen and reinforce the positive reasons. When the strengthened reasons for buying outweigh the reasons for not buying, the "maybe" changes to a "yes," and you make the sale. And you made the sale by making motivation work for you.

Understanding the Factors That Motivate

There are two basic kinds of motivation: positive (the kind that makes prospects say "yes!") and negative (the kind that makes prospects say "no!"). There is positive motivation when the prospect needs, wants, or likes what you are selling; in short, the prospect places positive values on it.

On the other hand, negative motivation comes from not needing, not wanting, or not liking whatever it is you are selling; and that means having an attitude toward it which places a low value on it.

Of course, the prospect may really want what you are selling. His or her reasons for not wanting your offering may be "real" or "unreal" and may be founded on ignorance, prejudice, false impressions, some kind of purely personal preference, etc. Whether or not those reasons are "good" reasons, you have to deal with them if you want to sell.

Remember, also, that most sales are made in competitive situations. The prospect may need, want, or like to buy "something like" what you want to sell. But there are other products or services "something like" (or, maybe to the prospect, "just like") yours. The buying decision will be made on a comparative basis; and the prospect will buy the offering that balances out with the highest total of the prospect's own positive values (including price).

Example: Selling the Positive Reasons

Tom Nesbit sells Ocelot automobiles. He has a prospect, Ronald Snedden, who is ready to buy either an Ocelot or the competitive Panther. Tom has learned that Mrs. Snedden puts a high value on appearance and interior luxury; he has also recognized that price is not a major consideration. When the Sneddens arrive for their third look (after their third look at a Panther), Tom shows them the most luxurious custom extras available in the Ocelot. Mrs. Snedden loves it, and Mr. Snedden buys it.

How did Tom make that sale? He figured that all the usual "benefits" that automobile salesmen push (engines, mileage, economy of servicing, etc.) were sufficiently similar in both the Ocelot and the Panther so that neither would be greatly valued over the other by the Sneddens. But, Tom also recognized that Mrs. Snedden placed a high value on luxury, style, and appearance (positive motivation for her). He figured he could offer enough of this in Ocelot's top-of-the-line model to outweigh any objection Mr. Snedden might have to the higher cost (negative motivation for him) with enough positive motivation left over to swing the decision to his Ocelot. And he was right.

This is an oversimplification of what happened. Tom Nesbit also used Motivational Selling Leverage to make the sale.

He used Motivational Selling Leverage to build a *relationship* with both the Sneddens, and that brought them back three times—not only to the Ocelot agency where he worked, but also to him.

He used Motivational Selling Leverage to build the most value for the Ocelot *benefits*, against the Panther *benefits*. And Tom did this in ways that were appropriate to each one of the Sneddens, in terms of the values that were important to them, individually.

He also used Motivational Selling Leverage to develop his *Communication* (his sales talk to them; his particularized "pitch") so it would not only be most acceptable and persuasive, but so that it would also be effective in emphasizing the benefits he was featuring and in building their confidence in him.

That kind of selling is the way most salespersons would like to sell, and would even try to sell, though it isn't as easy to do as it sounds. But Motivational Selling Leverage makes that kind of selling a lot easier.

The Principle of Leverage as Applied to Motivation

Motivational Leverage is based on the principle of the Lever. Look at Diagram 1-1. It shows:

The Lever itself

The Fulcrum on which it rests and works

The Force applied to it

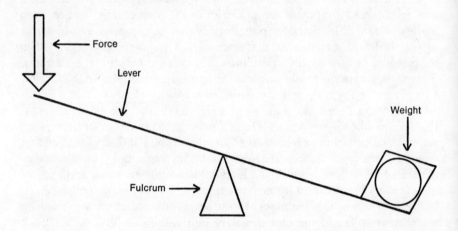

The Simple Mechanical Lever

Diagram 1-1

Leverage can be increased in three ways:

1. Move the Fulcrum closer to the Weight
2. Lengthen the Lever between Force and Fulcrum (the "Power Arm" of the Lever)
3. Increase the Force

Now, here is what is so very important about these three elements of leverage: they provide you with not one—not two—but *three* different ways to increase your leverage. And that fact applies, not only when you are using a lever to move an object, but also when you want to *motivate a prospect*. Just look at Diagram 1-2, and you'll understand.

Motivational Selling Leverage can be increased in three ways:

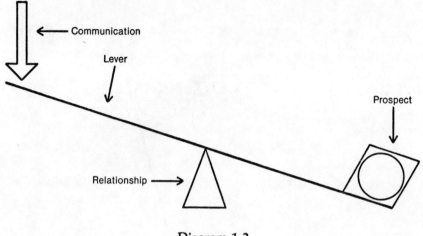

Diagram 1-2

1. Improve the *Relationship* with the Prospect (Fulcrum moves closer to weight)
2. Increase Prospect's perception of the value of *Benefits* (lengthens Power Arm of Lever)
3. Make *Communication* more effective (increase Force applied to Lever)

That's right! If you know how to do it, you can increase your Leverage—not only for moving things, but also for motivating prospects in *three* different ways—one for each of the three elements of leverage, mechanical or motivational.

(1) Improve your *Relationship* with the prospect, thereby moving the Fulcrum closer to the Weight (Diagram 1-3).

Chapter 6 tells you how to increase Motivational Selling Leverage by developing the right *Relationship* with the prospect.

(2) You can also improve your motivational leverage by offering *Benefits* of greater value to the prospect—thereby using a longer Lever arm (Diagram 1-4).

Chapter 2 tells you how to increase Motivational Selling Leverage by selling the *Benefits* which have the greatest motivational appeal to the prospect.

(3) You can *Communicate* more effectively, thereby applying more Force (Diagram 1-5).

Chapter 7 tells you how to use *Communication* with the prospect to exert the utmost motivational Force for making the sale.

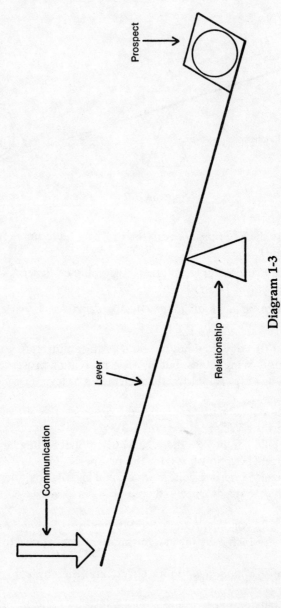

Diagram 1-3

(Same as 1-2, except lever arm longer, and Communication farther out.)

8

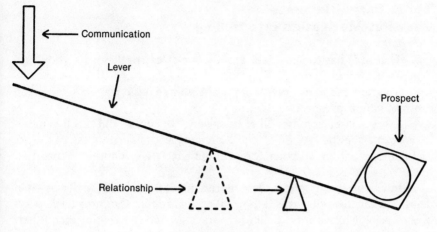

Diagram 1-4

(Same as 1-2, except indication that "Relationship" is moved closer to Prospect.)

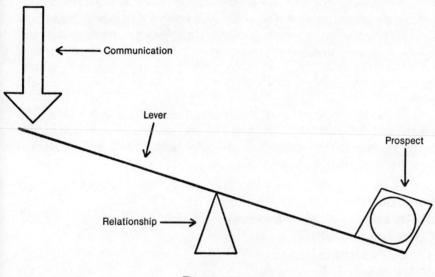

Diagram 1-5

(Same as 1-2, except Communication much bigger.)

You can gain an important selling-power advantage in any one of these three ways. You can also get *greater* leverage by combining two, or even three, of these advantages. *That* is exactly what Motivational Selling Leverage helps you to do: to apply *more leverage* to *motivate* the prospect to buy— from you!

Three Basic Elements
That Put Motivation into Selling

The three basic elements that motivate sales are these: *Relationship, Benefits, Communication.*

Diagram 1-2 shows you that there are three basic ways a salesperson can motivate a prospect.

Every salesperson uses all of these ways, of course, but this is generally done in a routine fashion, without an adequate understanding of the actual selling situation, and therefore without effectively adapting to the situation.

In Chapters 2, 6, and 7 these motivational factors will be discussed in detail. But at this point it is important to realize that the three basic ways of increasing Motivational Selling Leverage are independent of each other, and it is up to you to get them working together in the right combination to motivate the sale.

For instance: You may have an excellent relationship with the prospect, but that will not make the sale unless you have also emphasized benefits that the prospect values. Or, you may have a good relationship and have mentioned benefits the prospect values; but if you haven't done the right job of communicating, the prospect may not understand, may have missed an important point, may have taken something you said the wrong way, or may be unfavorably comparing what you say with somebody else's sales pitch.

If you understand the different motivational effects of these three elements, and the ways they relate and support one another, you will be able to put together the best possible combination of *Relationship, Benefits,* and *Communication* to make each sale.

How the Three Basic Elements of
Motivational Selling Leverage
Correspond to the
Three Basic Elements
of Mechanical Leverage

Prospects are motivated by their *Relationship* with the individual who is doing the selling and with the organization he or she represents. But remember: This is not the *Relationship* as *you* see it, but the *Relationship* as the *prospect sees it.*

This *Relationship* between salesperson and prospect corresponds to the position of the Fulcrum (look at Diagram 1-2 again) in both ordinary leverage and in Motivational Selling Leverage. If you have a *good Relationship* with the prospect, the Fulcrum can be very close to the weight, giving you added leverage. A salesperson can often keep moving that Fulcrum closer and closer to the weight, gaining more and more leverage. But the *Relationship* is only one of the three basic motivational factors. (Compare Diagrams 1-2 and 1-3.)

Now look at Diagram 1-2 again; and especially at the Power Arm— that part of the Lever that runs from the Fulcrum to where the Force is applied (on the other side of the Fulcrum from the weight).

Prospects (and customers) are motivated by their wants, needs, or likings (which come from their values). The *Benefits* represent the only selling points that can really motivate the sale, because they can provide satisfaction for the prospect's wants, needs or likings.

And the *Benefits*, with their values and attractiveness to the prospect, correspond to the length of the Lever (look at Diagram 1-4), which gives both mechanical advantage for ordinary leverage, and psychological advantage for Motivational Selling Leverage.

Prospects (and customers) are motivated by the *Communication* you use in selling. What you say, what you write, what you do, how you act and behave—the prospect reacts to all this; and it affects your *Relationship* with the prospect; and it also affects the way the prospect evaluates the *Benefits* you are selling—and the prospect is motivated by both of these results of your *Communication*. (Compare Diagrams 1-2 and 1-5.)

So the *Communication* you use in selling corresponds to the Force applied to the mechanical Lever in order to move the "weight"—in both ordinary leverage and in Motivational Selling Leverage.

How the Three Basic Elements of Motivational Selling Leverage Work Together

Remember—the most effective selling—and the most powerful Motivational Selling Leverage—can be yours if you use that combination of *Relationship*, *Benefits*, and *Communication* which is the very best you can put together for each sale.

Many salespersons "sell themselves"—they try to develop a personal relationship that will help them sell. Sometimes it works, and sometimes it doesn't.

Other salespersons go through a regular, routine explanation of the benefits without considering which benefits have value for the prospect. Almost always, then, they "sell" some benefits the prospect doesn't want to buy; and they don't do enough selling of the benefits the prospect values.

Some salespersons make the same "pitch" to every prospect—but the prospects may differ greatly in their needs. These needs cover such critical areas as familiarity with the product or service; knowledge of the competition; the time they have available to listen; their education, background and experience. No "standard pitch" can do a good job on every prospect—and especially not on the best prospects.

So if you want to develop the most positive motivation to buy, you should use the three basic motivational factors in that way which is best, and likely to be most effective, for each selling situation. You can do that if you understand how these three basic motivational factors work together (Diagram 1-6).

COMMUNICATION

RELATIONSHIP   BENEFITS

Diagram 1-6

This triangle suggests the way the three basic elements of selling interact with one another. Your *Communication* establishes and builds the *Relationship;* and *Communication* sells the *Benefits. Benefits* that provide satisfaction to the prospect improve the *Relationship* and increase confidence in your *Communication.* If you establish a good *Relationship,* it will influence the prospect's satisfaction with the *Benefits,* and it will increase the prospect's receptiveness to your *Communication.*

With the Motivational Selling Leverage System you can master the Power—the Motivation to Buy—that makes the prospect say "Yes!" You can do that because the Motivational Selling Leverage System tells you how to use and combine these *three* primary factors to create the most effective *motivation to buy*—from *you!*

Understanding the Values That Motivate the Buying Decision

Example: How to Lose a Sale

Newt Higbee works for Hermes Chemical Company, selling raw materials for compounding plastics. For years he has been trying to break into Global Plastics—the biggest user of the products Newt sells; but they have been tied up to his chief competitor, Major Chemicals.

Now, suddenly, his office has relayed a message from Link Noggle, chief purchasing agent with Global, asking Newt to drop by. Newt has been calling on Link for years, but has never gotten more than token or sample orders. Maybe this is the breakthrough Newt has long been hoping for.

In the waiting room outside Link's office Newt sees Doc Winslow, Nick Genaman, and Art Fuller—representatives of companies that are competitive with Newt's company. Newt remembers now that Major Chemicals, the primary supplier to Global, is having a strike. This means that Link is looking for a substitute supplier.

Called into Link's office, Newt goes into his usual routine about the purity of Hermes products, the care in compounding, the special protective (no loss) packaging, and the other benefits of the products he sells.

Finally, Link interrupts: "I know all that, Newt! Forget that. I'm only interested in your Plas-Mass, in bulk. How soon could you deliver six carloads?"

Newt pulls out a pad and pencil, and does a bit of calculating.

"That's 300 tons on a first order. You'd be entitled to a 4 percent discount for quantity, a 2 percent discount for bulk, and another 2 percent for a single shipment. You'd have to fill out a credit application, and there would be another 2 percent discount for payment within ten days of delivery. You can't beat those terms!"

Link draws a long breath. "Newt, I'm asking you again, how soon could we get delivery of six carloads?"

"Well, Link, it's like this. I'll draw up the order, and you sign it; and you get that application for credit OK'd by your treasurer and your bank, and send it to us. We'll requisition the boxcars as soon as those papers are in order, and our shipping department will figure the cheapest route."

"OK, Newt—that's about what I thought. Thanks for coming. On your way out, tell Doc Winslow to come on in."

Newt never did get the order. Several weeks later he ran into Doc Winslow in another waiting room and asked him if he was doing any business with Global's Link.

"You bet I am!" Doc gloated. "Right after Link called me into his office, he asked me how long it would take for us to deliver six carloads of Plas-Mass, in bulk. I called our factory on his phone, and they told me they were ready to ship from inventory. That was all there was to it. They started loading the boxcars while Link and I fixed up the paperwork. The cars rolled into their yard three days later, and we've been doing business with them ever since."

What Newt hadn't fully realized was that because of the strike at Major Chemicals, Link had to get the new shipments of Plas-Mass to the Global plant in time to avoid a shut-down. Therefore, the only benefit that interested Link was the quickest delivery.

But Newt didn't sell the one benefit that was important to Link. Newt was talking about discounts, credit, and payment, while Link was concerned about boxcars full of Plas-Mass rolling onto the siding of the Global plant— fast!

Doc Winslow caught onto Link's priorities immediately. He learned about the benefit that would control the buying decision for Link, and he sold *that Benefit*. He did it by getting a responsible, authoritative commitment from his own factory management; and by *Communicating* just the right message to Link. In doing so, he greatly improved his *Relationship* with Link and put himself in line for more orders.

This example illustrates the great importance of selling the benefits that will influence the buying decision; not just benefits, but benefits that have value for the prospect. Selling any other benefits may not only be a waste of time, but also of the opportunity to sell the right benefits for the particular selling situation.

All right, then—how *do* you know which benefits to sell? There is no one answer to this question. Discovering the best benefit to sell is not always easy, but there is nothing more essential to effective selling.

Basically there are two ways to know what benefits to sell. One way involves all the possible sources other than the prospect. (Newt Higbee should have known about the strike at Major, and should have foreseen the opportunity to fill the gap.)

The other way, of course, does involve the prospect directly. Often, it is best to rely on a combination of both. This usually means doing some finding out or research before you meet the prospect, so you can deal far more intelligently and informedly with the prospect. In other kinds of relationships you may find it advantageous to do some further investigating after you have talked to the prospect—following up leads and ideas gained from the prospect and building up your *Communication* to sell most effectively the *Benefits* you have found to be most pertinent.

Your *Relationship* with the prospect is the primary key to learning from him or her what *Benefits* are of interest. Most people will respond well to intelligent questions about matters that interest them—especially about matters that have value for them—their needs and wants; and especially if the questions are intelligently posed and followed up and indicate a constructive interest on the part of someone who is (or may be) in a position to satisfy those needs and wants.

Of course, the better your *Relationship*, the more you can learn about the prospect's values and the better you can individualize your selling. Thus the right *Relationship* not only puts your Fulcrum closer to the weight, but can also give you a longer Lever arm and more forceful *Communication*—if you know how to use Motivational Selling Leverage.

★ ★ 2 ━━━━━━━━━━━━━━━ ★ ★
How Selling Leverage
Gives You the Sharp,
Smart Selling Advantage

Four Basic Principles of Selling

Practically everyone who knows anything about selling agrees there are four principles or rules that determine its effectiveness. These principles are fundamental; they apply to *all* selling, from "opening" to "closing." If you observe them, you will have a good chance of making the sale.

There is a problem, however. The rules look simple, but living up to them is not simple. The problem is complicated because the rules seem to contradict one another.

The four basic principles are these:

1. Sell your product or service by selling the benefits.
2. Sell your product or service by "selling yourself."
3. Standardize your selling; always use proven sales arguments and techniques.
4. Individualize your selling; personalize your sales talk by fitting it to the needs, wants, interests, and values of each customer.

Clearly, all four rules are sound; but it is also clear that the first two rules seem to contradict one another, and so do the last two.

Should you concentrate on selling the benefits? Or should you sell yourself? And how can you do both? If you use proven sales arguments, how can you individualize your selling?

The answer is to utilize the best possible combination of the principles. This is not easy unless you use Motivational Selling Leverage, which was especially created to help find and apply the right combination of principles for each selling situation.

In any selling situation, there are many factors involved—too many for even the most competent and experienced salespeople to recognize and understand; so, they usually try to deal with only those factors which they think will have the greatest motivational effect, and to do this in ways that seem best at the time, or which are most natural—and therefore easiest—for them to use.

Some salespeople are successful because they are able to sell the benefits effectively, while others make many sales by "selling themselves." Some use standardized selling, while others individualize their selling for each prospect. How well each of them succeeds with these different ways of selling depends on many factors, some of which are:

1. The kinds of products or services they are selling.

2. The kinds of prospects or customers to whom they are selling.

3. Their own individual personalities.

4. The personalities of individual prospects.

5. Their knowledge of and experience with the product or service, and with the market.

But each prospect or customer is different; therefore, every sale is different. Consequently, the salesperson has to arrive at a particular way of motivating a prospect to say "Yes!" That calls for the right combination of the basic principles of selling to fit the particular combination of factors involved. That means, to motivate each sale, there must be a different combination of selling methods.

By now, you may begin to feel that the subject of motivating sales is very complicated. Well, it is true that motivations can be complex. When motivating someone to buy, many factors may be involved that need careful attention, if you are to make the sale. Therefore, what is needed is help in doing this better—which means, making it easier.

Motivational Selling Leverage does make it easy for you to handle such situations by applying the Four Basic Selling Principles most effectively to each prospect, in ways that fit your own natural selling style.

You Can "Sell the Benefits" by Applying Motivational Selling Leverage to the First Basic Principle of Selling

The first—and probably the most basic—principle of selling tells us to *sell the benefits*. That sounds obvious and sensible. Who could argue with that?

Example: A Simple Selling Situation

CUSTOMER: (*To Dick Embree, Drugstore Clerk*) I need something for a headache.

DICK: This is Paingo. It really fixes headaches.

CUSTOMER: That's just what I need! I'll take it. How much is it?

In this situation, the customer declares a need, and the salesperson presents a product which he says can meet that need. Meeting that need is the only benefit the customer is interested in. By stating that the offered product meets that need, the salesperson is selling the benefit that counts in this particular selling situation. A closer, more favorable relationship isn't necessary. The customer has asked the salesperson to provide a product that can meet his or her need. This communication is important, because the salesperson has to identify the offered product as capable of meeting the customer's need; it is very simple, and no real selling is required here.

But most selling situations aren't as simple and easy as that. Compare that situation with this one:

Example: Meeting the Customer's Needs

CUSTOMER: (*To Dick Embree*) I have a bad headache, and I need something for it right away.

DICK: How about some Paingo? That will clear up your headache fast.

CUSTOMER: Does it contain aspirin? I'm allergic to salicilates.

DICK: Let's see. Well, the label says it contains some aspirin. . . . Now, here's Kurake. The label says—look here—contains no aspirin.

CUSTOMER: OK, but what'll it do to my blood pressure? Some of these over-the-counter remedies have warnings about that.

DICK: Yes—and here it is, so . . . no Kurake. Let me see. (*Calls*) Mr. Gringle! (*to Customer*) Mr. Gringle is our pharmacist. He'll know what to give you.

GRINGLE: Can I help?

DICK: This gentleman has a headache, but he's allergic to aspirin, so I can't give him Paingo; and he has high blood pressure, so I can't give him Kurake. What would you recommend?

GRINGLE: Well, you could try Sufferno, or Agonot, or—let me think—maybe Hurtaway. Ever try any of those?

CUSTOMER: I tried Hurtaway once—it gave me acid stomach.

GRINGLE: Well, that leaves Sufferno and Agonot.

CUSTOMER: How much are they?

GRINGLE: (*Holds up product*) This is Sufferno; it's $3.89.

CUSTOMER: What! For that little bit? How many tablets does it have?

GRINGLE: Twenty-four in this size Sufferno; that's about 16¢ a tablet—not much to pay to cure a bad headache. We also have the large size container; that's 100 tablets for only $12.98—about 13¢ apiece.

CUSTOMER: How about that other one—Agonot?

GRINGLE: This is the smallest package that Agonot comes in. It's only $1.79 for 12 tablets—that's about 15¢ each. And, we have the family size.

CUSTOMER: Is Agonot just as good as Sufferno?

GRINGLE: Yes, it's the same formula, except that Sufferno is made by Zip Pharmaceutical and Agonot by Zap Drugs. Either one'll ease your headache; and this package of Agonot will ease 12 headaches for only $1.79.

CUSTOMER: OK—I'll take it.

Now, that *wasn't* so simple, was it? The customer not only wanted something to cure his headache, he also wanted a remedy that didn't contain salicilates, that wouldn't affect his high blood pressure, and that wasn't too expensive. Whoever sold him a remedy would have to find out the specifics of his need, and offer him the benefits that would meet his special requirements.

This selling situation was too much for Dick, the drugstore clerk, but not too much for Gringle, a qualified, licensed pharmacist. This illustrates another important point: To sell the benefits effectively, you can't know too much about the kinds of needs people may have, and you can't know too much about the ways those needs can be met by what you want to sell.

In the process of making this sale, Dick had to withdraw from the relationship he had begun with the customer, because he knew he didn't know enough to give the customer what he needed. Gringle began the relationship with the customer by being introduced as a pharmacist—an expert who could handle what Dick could not. Gringle built the relationship by providing precise information to meet the customer's needs and cost concerns, until there was an effective match between the customer's needs and concerns, and the benefits of a particular item that Gringle was offering.

Of course, the communication applied by Gringle was more informative than Dick had needed in the first example and far beyond what Dick could have provided in the second example.

In the second example, the sale was made by a combination of *Relationship* and *Communication* supporting the sale of the *Benefits*—a good example of how Motivational Selling Leverage works when applied to the first and most basic principle of selling: *Sell the Benefits*.

Although the sale was a small one, and perhaps scarcely worth Gringle's time, it is likely that that customer will be back—especially if he wants to have a doctor's prescription filled or if he needs further advice on over-the-counter pharmaceuticals.

These examples were simple and involved comparatively easy retail sales of standard package goods. Here is an example on selling "big ticket" consumer durables.

Example: Applying Motivational Selling Leverage by Selling Benefits

Reggie Nollins sells powered lawnmowers, wholesale—mostly to hardware stores and to home and garden supply houses. He has a lot of competition; each competitive brand and model has certain features, at certain prices. Reggie sells machines that have competitive features at competitive prices—but they certainly do not outclass the competition.

Reggie sells the benefits—but he has a particular way of selling the benefits that gives him a big Motivational Selling Leverage advantage. Reggie makes a particular effort to talk to the salespeople—not just to the owner, the manager, or the buyer. Reggie sells the benefits of his powered lawnmowers in such a way that the salespeople learn how effectively they can sell them to *their* customers.

Reggie really knows how to sell the benefits of his powered lawnmowers. When the store's salespeople listen to him, they soon catch on to how *they* can sell those same benefits to the people who come into their store. When they believe they can sell Reggie's lawnmowers successfully, those are the lawnmowers they want to sell.

The salespeople depend on Reggie for that kind of help in their own selling; and they really appreciate the help Reggie gives them. That creates an important kind of *Relationship* for Reggie's selling. Also, Reggie *Communicates* well in selling the *Benefits* of his lawnmowers. So, when it comes to leverage, Reggie not only has a well-placed Fulcrum and a rather potent Force, but—most important—a fairly long Lever. Reggie's lawnmowers keep moving out of the store because the salespeople know how to sell the benefits.

You Can "Sell Yourself" More Effectively by Applying Motivational Selling Leverage to the Second Basic Principle of Selling

The secret of the second basic principle of selling is not only to "sell yourself," but *to create the right Relationship.*

Individuals always react, more or less favorably or unfavorably, to contacts with other people. Such reactions are quite involuntary—you can't help having *some* reaction to people you talk to. Such reactions, of course, affect the relationship between people, even when that relationship is limited to a single contact, or when the relationship is not important. In a sense, it is a "natural" human trait to want to "sell yourself," and most of us do it often in both selling and nonselling situations.

All salespeople should understand the concept of relationships. Ordinarily, when we talk about a relationship, we are thinking in terms of an ongoing interaction between two people, as in a marriage or love affair; or in a partnership or a close friendship; or among co-workers, or between workers and their boss; or between relatives; or some other significant, continuing connection between individuals. Those are the kinds of relationships that are important to us, personally.

But let us also think, for a moment, of what we call "business relationships" (other than those suggested above). Some of these are "strictly business"—there is nothing "personal" or "social" about them. Others are "mixed"—the personal and social are mixed in with doing business.

People who work together often entertain one another, and any "business lunch" has something of a personal, social angle. Many salespersons use hospitality to "warm up" prospects and to entertain their customers, and to get to know one another better; while others usually deal rather formally with customers. Many salespeople have long-standing, friendly relations with their customers; others operate on the basis of a single meeting. Whether you and your family have been spending vacations with a customer and his or her family for years, or you are seeing a prospect for the first time, there is a *Relationship* between you, and it must have *some* effect on your selling.

It is true that some purchasers deal with salespersons they actively dislike when they have reasons for so dealing, which outweigh their aversion. Purchasers do not always buy from the salesperson they like most; again, other reasons affect their buying decisions.

There is no question that a favorable relationship helps a sale, and an unfavorable relationship handicaps it; and that is true whether the relationship has been developed over years of friendly meetings, or has just begun with a cold-call self-introduction. That is why your *Relationship* with the prospect or customer serves as the Fulcrum of Motivational Selling Leverage.

Salespeople know about this, at least intuitively, and many of them do a lot of self-selling to develop a relationship that they think will support their selling. "Selling yourself" can be a effective tactic. However, it can also lead to results that are the opposite of what you intended; and the only way to avoid that is to know—for each selling situation—*if* you should do it, *when* you should do it, and *how* you should do it. Motivational Selling Leverage can help you to judge that *if, when* and *how* of selling yourself, so that you can not only "sell yourself," but also create a *Relationship* with the prospect that is the right one for making the sale.

For instance, just being liked—having a personal relationship with a customer that is primarily social or based on entertainment—can be helpful in many ways. It can sometimes get you in to make a call when the customer is busy and other salespersons are waiting. It can give you a decisive edge in the buying decision. In a sales contact with a stranger, making a "pleasing impression" can keep a conversation going longer, giving you a better chance to make the sale. (Of course, if you like the person you are dealing with, the whole experience becomes more pleasant for you.)

Example: Selling Yourself Is Not Enough

Rod McFee competes with Reggie Nollins; they both sell powered lawn-mowers, wholesale. You can't help liking Rod, and everybody is glad to see him walk in. He has a joke or a gift for everyone—a cigar, a lipstick, a souvenir, or some kind of trick or "gag."

Rod sells a line that has been around a long time, and he has a good reputation. But he doesn't put in much time selling the benefits.

Rod used to do quite well, because he got a lot of leverage from the positioning of the Fulcrum—his *Relationships* were good for that. Customers still come in and ask for the make of machine that Rod sells, because they have had it before, or they have heard about it from friends or neighbors.

But in the last few years, there have been some new models and new technology in the power lawnmower field, and there are many new benefits to sell. And in time, many of the "oldtimers" who knew and liked Rod have gone, and those who have taken their place are not as easy for Rod to charm.

So now Rod needs more Motivational Selling Leverage than he is getting from his *Relationships.* He is trying to sell differently, particularly in places where he isn't that popular. In such places he *does* talk about the *Benefits.* Rod is learning. It is a hard lesson for him to learn, but he understands that just "selling yourself," being liked, is not enough.

Relationships that are good for selling often call for much more than being liked. Fundamentally, there are three characteristics that many prospects and customers look for in salespeople, and they usually have good reason to value—and expect—these characteristics. Therefore, the best way to "sell yourself" is to *demonstrate* that you possess these characteristics, by selling in such a way that the prospect recognizes that you have them. Those three prime characteristics for selling yourself are: *being helpful, being knowledgeable,* and *building confidence.*

But you can't build confidence without reliability. Can you be counted on? When you say you will do something, will you do it? To develop a reputation for reliability, you must prove that you are reliable by living up to the obligations you undertake. If you say you will secure certain information and will call back with it, be sure to do it. Make certain, for example, that the pricing and delivery data, specifications, and shipping instructions are followed. Remember, it is very easy to build a reputation for *not* being reliable. All you have to do is fail once!

There is also loyalty. Successful salespeople build relationships of mutual loyalty with their customers. Such loyalty involves certain expectations: the customer expects the fullest benefits of any discounts, lower prices, or special concessions; also, the highest priority and the best possible service for repairs, returns, spare parts, installation, deliveries, etc.; as well as the earliest and most complete information, not only on the product or service you are selling, but on anything else that may be of interest to the customer. You can build yourself up as a loyal supporter of the customer's position in his company by showing that you understand what interests him, and that you have his interest in mind and really want to be helpful.

There is a famous quotation (from Emerson) that goes like this: ". . . What you are . . . thunders so loudly that I cannot hear what you say. . . ." This is another way of saying that people are judged by their actions more than by their words: "By their deeds shall ye know them."

So, the most effective way to sell yourself is by doing and not by talking. When you try to sell yourself by telling the prospect or customer positive things about yourself, he is likely to be skeptical or not interested. But when you build your relationship on being helpful, truthful, reliable, and loyal, your customer is likely to act in the same manner toward you.

When you have a customer who perceives you in this way, you will have a *Relationship* that moves the Fulcrum close to the weight and, therefore, you will have a considerable selling leverage (even when you may be weak on *Benefits* and *Communication*).

Motivational Selling Leverage can help you to build that kind of *Relationship*.

How to Use Your Knowledge to Create a Solid Foundation for a Selling Relationship

Being Helpful

If there is one basic requirement for establishing the right kind of *Relationship* with a prospect or customer, it is to be helpful. That means, helping them to make the best buying decision, and helping them generally. But you cannot be helpful without being knowledgeable, nor can you be helpful to anyone who does not have confidence in you.

If the prospect knows less than you do about the product or service, the competition, the market, the applications, the relevant background, developments, trends, etc., then he will want to learn this from you. If you can establish yourself as a good, reliable source of information, you will have an excellent base for a *Relationship* that can help you to sell.

You will be engaged in conversations in which you inform one another of matters that each of you has learned about since your previous meeting;

and you can gain information that you could get in no other way, which could be extremely valuable to selling there and elsewhere. Each meeting should strengthen the *Relationship*—*if* you "sell yourself" by knowing what interests the prospect.

On the other hand, if the prospect or customer knows more than you do about the product or service, the competition, etc., he or she will probably not want to spend any more time with you than they think necessary.

There is a way to salvage such situations. You must be frank: "I'm new with this company. I was with International Glucose, but I switched to Malleable Glass because I thought that the industries we sell to are more interesting. I'd appreciate any information or advice you care to offer." Few people can resist an opportunity to show how well informed they are, particularly when their specialty is involved. If you show genuine appreciation, remember what you have been told, and refer to it now and then, you can build a *Relationship* in which the prospect takes a continuing interest in your progress. But you have to listen, learn, and apply what you learn.

Building Confidence

There are several kinds of confidence valued by prospects and customers, which you can build up in them by what you do.

First, there is truth, veracity, honesty. Any deviation from this—or anything perceived as a deviation—will destroy a relationship. Customers like to deal with people they can trust. Along with this goes confidence in your accuracy. You can make an "honest mistake" without destroying confidence in your basic honesty, but people do feel more confidence in people who are careful to be accurate.

How Motivational Selling Leverage Helps You Sell More Successfully by Applying the Best Combination of the First and Second Basic Principles of Selling

If you sell the benefits without selling yourself, you are sacrificing what could be important additional power to your selling leaverage. If you sell yourself without selling the benefits, you are wasting the considerable advantage of a Fulcrum that is close to the weight. Yet, most salespersons handicap themselves by over- or underemphasizing these important selling tactics.

Benefits are beneficial to the prospect only if they have value to him or her; and when you are *knowledgeable* enough to know what has value to the prospect, then you can be *helpful* in pointing this out, and relating those *Benefits* to the prospect's values. That is the only truly effective way to "sell the benefits," and you can do it if you have learned enough about the prospect to be helpful, and not simply to give a "canned talk" on benefits.

Even if what you say could be helpful, it will not make much of an impression if the prospect has little or no confidence in you, does not perceive you as helpful or knowledgeable, does not know you to be truthful, reliable, and willing to develop a *Relationship* of mutual loyalty.

How do you get to the point where you derive top selling leverage by applying the best combination of the two principles, "sell the benefits" and "sell yourself"? How do you put them together to gain the maximum benefits of both?

Basically, the answer is: Sell yourself by the way you sell the benefits.

Sell yourself as helpful by selling the benefits in a way the prospect perceives as helpful to him or her and his or her organization.

Sell yourself as knowledgeable by selling the benefits in a way the prospect perceives as demonstrating, not only your knowledge of the product or service, but also its potential applications that are or may be of interest to the prospect.

As a salesperson with a prospect, it is natural for you, and expected of you, to sell the benefits of the product or service you represent. So you have a wide-open opportunity to show how helpful and how knowledgeable you are.

But the other important components of a good *Relationship* are not so readily demonstrated. Most prospects will not perceive you as truthful, reliable, and loyal because you say you are. You have to win confidence over time and develop a reputation for honesty and sincerity by your conduct.

Many relationships between salespersons and their prospects provide ample opportunity for the participants to evaluate one another and to distinguish qualities in one another not readily apparent in a routine sales call. Many mutually beneficial relationships have grown up between salespeople and customers. Such relationships are a major source of the satisfaction that the occupation of selling has to offer.

As you build the *Relationship* by creating the perception that you are both knowledgeable and helpful, you can also build the *Relationship* in other ways.

Sell yourself as an individual worthy of confidence in the only way that really counts—by earning it, by inviting opportunities to demonstrate it, and by justifying those opportunities.

Sell yourself as truthful by being truthful; as reliable by being reliable; as loyal by being loyal.

Establish your credentials: refer to customers; cite your education, your background; your experience; establish your expertise on any basis that is valid and that the prospect will respect. Remember: Every minute you spend talking about yourself is a minute taken away from talking about the product or service you are there to sell. Be sure you are making the best use of that time for the purpose that brought you there: not to sell yourself, but to sell your product or service.

When it comes to conversation about matters unrelated to business, be sure it supports the *Relationship*, and is not something you are doing because it is easier, more pleasant, or more satisfying *to you*.

Chapter 6 includes a discussion on how to develop selling leverage when you are socializing with customers.

How Motivational Selling Leverage Helps You to Apply the Third Basic Principle of Selling

In applications of Motivational Selling Leverage, the Force that acts upon the Lever is *Communication*. The third basic principle of selling is that we should *Communicate* by using language which has been proven to be effective.

Some kinds of organization, by the very nature of their marketing, emphasize the use of standardized language in the selling activities of their representatives. In many such cases, a great deal of survey, research, and years of organizational experience have gone into the development of "openings" and other major components of the standardized selling pattern in which salespeople are trained.

Let us consider the kinds of products and services that are most effectively salable in this way; the kinds of marketing organizations that have such a policy, the kinds of selling situations in which standardized "patter" can be most useful and effective; and the implications of this for other kinds of products and services, and for other kinds of selling situations.

First, the kinds of products and services that have been most successfully marketed door-to-door, on a house-to-house, apartment-to-apartment, one call only, cold-call basis. These include such diverse lines as brushes, cooking utensils, vacuum cleaners, cosmetics, jewelry, encyclopedias and other books, and a variety of other commodities and supplies (not to mention magazine subscriptions!) which are generally marketed by nationwide organizations, often supported by national advertising, thus having names that are likely to be recognized. Their marketing plans call for virtually every household in the country to be contacted—literally many millions of individual calls.

Other national marketing organizations target businesses—any kind (for office supplies, equipment of wide application, etc.), or certain kinds with known, special needs, as well as retailers or distributors of certain categories and lines of product.

To accomplish their objectives, such organizations set up an organizational hierarchy, beginning with the headquarters group, and usually descending (for example) to regions, states, districts (cities, towns, counties), sub-districts, and territories.

In reverse order, a territory consists of an area considered to hold about the right number of households for one sales representative to cover within a certain time-frame. A sub-district consists of about as many territories as one local official can supervise. A district consists of about as many sub-districts as its manager can handle; and there are executives at the state level to manage the districts; and senior executives over the regions to manage the states. Thus, there are four levels (in the example presented here) between the headquarters people and the individual sales representative assigned to a territory.

Beginning with the states and with the hundreds of districts within the states, we easily arrive at thousands of sub-districts, and perhaps 20 times that many territories. In fact, some companies that market in this way may have hundreds of thousands of representatives (many of them part-time). They, of course, are recruited locally by the sub-district supervisor, who has been selected (probably from among the more promising territorial representatives) by the District Manager. Certainly, some of the territorial representatives recruited have a high potential, while others are incompetent, poorly motivated, or otherwise ineffective. Some dress well; others do not. Some are polite and well-spoken; others are rude in manners and speech. Some are favorably known in their territorial neighborhoods; others are not, and so on. The people in headquarters won't know anything about such "remote" details; these will be buried in the broad generalities of reports from the executives at the regional, and perhaps at the state, level.

So headquarters develops doctrine for the recruitment, training, and supervision of the territorial representatives by the sub-district supervisors, and expects the district managers to follow-up to obtain the best results. Thus, the best and worst territorial representatives receive training and instruction handed down from the same source, training that usually includes such specific requirements as an opening ("Hello! I'm your neighborhood Glitch representative, and I have a gift for you."), the answers to certain (anticipated) questions, and the precise procedures for conducting demonstrations, or for the detailed exposition of offers, and especially, how to sell the benefits.

Obviously, some individuals need such training more than others. For some salespersons, strict adherence to what they have learned may make the difference between failure and success; while for others, it could constitute a handicap. But the overall value of this kind of training cannot be denied.

Let us also consider the sales activities of local enterprises. The door-to-door solicitations of neighborhood tradespeople (laundries, pest exterminators, lawn care, snow removal, etc.) are often made by the principals of such businesses or by their associates. They may start off with a standard "spiel," but their responses to questions and household comments are spontaneous and knowledgeable. They are likely to sell the benefits effectively, since they are knowledgeable about local conditions.

In time, such local businesspeople develop their own standard sales talk, but they develop it themselves.

Neighborhood representatives of national marketing organizations develop a selling *Relationship* by making regular calls. Here the organizational functioning tends to be tightened up: recruitment aims at qualified individuals; training is more extensive, intensive, and continuous; new products and special offers are added from time to time; and supervision is more attentive, exacting, and constructive.

The representatives develop personal *Relationships* with their customers. They sell the *Benefits* of the products they offer in terms suggested by company literature and training. But their *Communication* tends to be adapted to each *Relationship*, borrowing standard language mainly to provide information about products and terms.

Let us skip from this stage of salespersonship to that of the salesperson who calls on particular prospects: purchasing agents, retail store buyers, and professionals (engineers, architects, doctors, etc.). Many of these salespeople make calls at regular intervals (once a week, once a month, once every six weeks), and they establish a substantial *Relationship*. They are often told by their managements to "push" certain products at certain times or seasons; and they are usually provided with special information and training. They are expected to adapt what they learn to each selling situation.

All of this discussion is intended to help you orient your own situation among the perspectives offered and to help you decide whether and how you should use "proven sales language."

You should arrive at that decision by knowing what will help you exert a maximum of Motivational Selling Leverage, by providing the *Communication* that best supplements your *Relationship* with the customer, and that provides the best way to sell the *Benefits*.

How Motivational Selling Leverage Helps You to Apply the Fourth Basic Principle of Selling

Some people know exactly what they want, and they'll buy from you if the price and other considerations are competitive and acceptable. If they already want what you have, you don't have to sell the *Benefits*. If the prospect is already sold, then your *Communication* probably won't matter very much; and your *Relationship* also may not matter at all (or it may have been the deciding factor).

In cases of impulse buying, again, the customer has been attracted by some perceived benefit, and there's little additional need for selling.

But in between these two extremes of ready-made buying decisions there are many kinds of situations where the right kind of selling will make the crucial difference. Essentially, this requires the salesperson to find out what values will influence the prospect to buy and then to sell the *Benefits* that appeal to those values. The *Relationship* should help you to learn about those values and what *Benefits* to emphasize in your selling. Your *Communication* determines how effectively you sell the *Benefits* that you believe relate to those values.

Clearly, this way of looking at the process of selling emphasizes the need for individualized selling, since each prospect will be influenced by different values. (By "values," we mean those considerations that can influence the buying decision, as discussed in Chapter 1.)

To illustrate this point, here is an example of the opportunity for more effective Motivational Selling Leverage by individualizing the selling of power lawnmowers.

Example: Why Ken Bradley Demanded Individualized Selling

Ken Bradley owns and manages Bradley Home and Garden Supply in Prenticeville, Ohio, which carries a full line of power lawnmowers. Ken called a meeting of all his salespeople, and here is what he said to them:

"You all know we have pretty stiff competition from Supreme Hardware—not to mention Sears, Wards, and those other big mail-order and shopping mall outfits. We are losing a lot of sales we could have made, because we don't individualize our selling. So, we need to make our selling fit the individual customer.

"You are all using the standard sales arguments based on the manufacturers' literature, and they are OK, as far as they go. But you have to make them fit what the individual customer wants. Most of you are not doing that.

"For instance, a woman comes in about a week ago and asks Joe, here, for a Rex—the kind that Rod McFee sells us. What does Joe do? He gives her the old spiel that Rod always gives us—that old "leader of the industry," "old reliable," "first to put power into lawn-mowing" kind of selling. What happens? She tells Joe she'd just like to look around a bit; and she goes over to the lawnmower display and examines different models there. Then she walks out.

"Well, it just so happens that the woman's house is down the street from my son's, and I saw her yesterday, operating a Rex on her lawn. Why didn't she buy that Rex from us? I wanted to know that; so I went up to her and asked her.

"She told me that her neighbor had recommended a Rex, but she didn't know what size or model to buy. When she looked at our display she realized that she had quite a range of choices, and would need some expert advice—but she figured she wouldn't be getting that from Joe, the way he was spouting that standard stuff. So she went down to Supreme Hardware, and their salesman asked her how big her lawn is, how often she mows it, whether she has a lot of leaves falling on it, and lots of other questions like that. Then he recommended Rex Model C—and she bought it! Now, that's what I call *individualized* selling! And that's what I want *all of you* to be doing!"

Perhaps no industry has studied the art and science of selling as extensively as the life insurance business. For many years its primary "product" was "straight life," with a few modifications and options. Then some of the smarter salespeople realized that the *real* value of life insurance to the buyer is not only the money the company will pay when the insured dies, but the way the company can take care of the insured's survivors, as a part of the total estate the insured expects to leave. That realization led to the idea of *estate planning*, in which the salesperson collects detailed information about the assets the prospect plans to leave, exactly what he or she wants to do with those assets, and how he or she would like to provide for each beneficiary.

Of course, such information is different for each prospect; and so each estate plan must be different. But each estate plan shows exactly how life insurance can best help to carry out the prospect's wishes.

This is an example of marketing through individualized selling techniques; in fact, the salesperson who sells estate planning often educates the prospect, and even helps him or her to figure out what he or she wants to accomplish in making a last will and testament.

Estate planning probably represents an extreme of individualized selling and of special *Relationship* between prospect and salesperson. However, there are many selling situations that offer similar opportunities for individualized selling.

Let us take an example of individualized selling that is far removed from estate planning. Let us take your neighborhood vendor of ice creams.

Example: Tim, the Street Vendor

The product—ice cream—is well known, and a demand is already established. Tim appears (with bicycle-driven refrigerated container) and eager customers gather, and make their wants known. Some call out for particular treats they have enjoyed before or that have been recommended; others review the signs on the vehicle that advertise the different flavors and coatings, and that announce the specials.

Business is brisk, and there seems to be little need for the vendor to sell the benefits or even to communicate. People hold out their money and call out their choice. The transaction may easily end with no words uttered by the vendor. However, his sales objectives are usually met. He sells out, even leaves behind some unsatisfied demand, and he'll be back next time with a larger stock.

What can Motivational Selling Leverage do to increase the selling success of this vendor?

Tim is a pleasant chap who likes youngsters, smiles easily, and has a good memory. He soon remembers faces and buying preferences, and he even anticipates some demands by holding out a desired item with such remarks as "Here's your Nutty Goo Pistachio Splendor, Ludwig; I saved it for you!" or "Hi, Selena—I love to hand a Strawberry Walnut Super to a pretty girl—especially when it almost matches her hair!" or "I had to hide those Chocolate Angel Tempters from the gang at Maple and Elm—I wanted to save them for the guys on the team that beat Central."

Tim has made himself a kind of neighborhood institution, known and accepted by all the children and their parents. Furthermore, his attention to "who wants what" enables him to stock up for each day with the product mix that is most likely to sell out.

Tim has built a *Relationship* that puts the Fulcrum close to the weight, by using individualized conversation with his customers. Given the ready-made demand, he scarcely needs his occasional efforts at selling the *Benefits*, which may range from "I ate one of these Chocolate North Pole Celebrations myself, before I started out. Boy-oh-boy! was it terrific! How did you like yours, Archie?" to "Sorry, I'm all out of Dream-Jacketed Cherry Ideals—I'll bring plenty tomorrow. How about a Supreme Vanilla Pecan Reward instead? They're terrific, too."

Tim gets his Motivational Selling Leverage from the *Relationship* he has developed by service and *Communication*, while doing everything necessary to support the largely self-selling *Benefits* of his product.

How to Individualize
Your Selling

Now compare Tim's selling with that of Hans, who works in the Regal Restaurant, downtown.

Example: Hans, the Waiter, and Today's Specials

The Regal Restaurant has a printed menu bound in a plastic cover, and it lists a number of standard dishes. There are also two kinds of daily specials: "regular" specials are listed on the menu and are served on a certain day of the week (Mondays, roast chicken, pot-roast; Tuesdays, ham, veal; Wednesdays, calves' liver, turkey; Thursdays, beef stew, pork chops; etc.).

"Daily Specials" are usually decided on the night before by the owner and the chef, according to the items available in the market. These are listed on a separate piece of paper and clipped to the regular menu; they may range from "Blue Fish" or "Smelts" to "Club Steak" or "Risotto."

The demand for such Daily Specials is unpredictable, yet a matter of concern to the owner. He watches the orders and the dwindling and undwindling supplies. At a given moment the owner will decide that he must take action. Sometimes a menu item is sold out, which delights the owner. If it is a "Daily Special," he is especially delighted.

In the case of the undwindling items, it is quite another story. The owner soon becomes concerned about the threatened oversupply of the expensive perishables that back up various entries on the menu and make up the "Daily Specials." Something must be done to avoid such costly waste, and the logical option is to promote the lagging sales of the less favored items. The task of selling the abundant items, and especially the "Daily Specials," falls to the waiters, who are soon told which items to "recommend."

Hans has been a waiter in this restaurant a long time. He has his own regular customers, who sit at his tables, and ask his suggestions about what they should order; and they often do as he suggests. Hans also acknowledges his obligation to the owner—to help sell off the slow-selling Daily Specials. But he also knows there is always the possibility of a conflict of interest: if he recommends a Daily Special that his customers do not like, his *Relationship* with them will suffer. They will blame him for suggesting something they did not enjoy, and will lose faith in his recommendations. They may even suspect that he betrayed their faith in him by pushing an item on them, merely to sell it. He and the restaurant may lose a regular customer. He recognizes that he would be sacrificing a good relationship, with long-term selling value, in order to make an immediate sale of only temporary value to the owner.

Hans is no fool. He has had this kind of problem before, and he knows how to compromise. He will mention the Daily Special, but he will make several other suggestions; and it will be difficult to detect any particular emphasis in his recommendations.

"Mrs. Blauvelt, I know that you like veal, and we have it several ways—roast veal, Wiener schnitzel, Veal Parmigiano; and Mr. Blauvelt, you like seafood. Well, we have all the seafood listed on the menu, plus a special today, bluefish. What shall I tell the chef to prepare for you?"

Clever Hans: he reinforced his *Relationship* with the Blauvelts by demonstrating his knowledge of their individual tastes; he identified the items that related to such tastes; but he avoided identifying himself with a special recommendation for any one item.

Hans demonstrated a special kind of individualized selling: he carefully avoided selling any particular *Benefits* and kept his *Communication* to a minimum, in order not to jeopardize a *Relationship* of some importance for the future.

Many a salesperson embarrassed by instructions that do not fit the specific selling situation could take a cue from this kind of individualized selling.

Making the Best Combination of the Third and Fourth Basic Principles of Selling

It is important to understand the advantages you can gain from using proven selling language, and those you can gain from individualizing your selling; and it is important to realize that these two ways of selling, as prescribed by the third and fourth principles of successful selling, are not contradictory and can be combined into successful Motivational Selling Leverage. Usually, such combinations individualize the selling by selecting the benefits that will have the greatest appeal (value) for the prospect, and using the proven selling language to sell those benefits.

Ken Bradley told his lawnmower salespeople about individualizing their selling. Here's what he told them about using standard selling arguments.

Example: The Right Way to Use Standardized Sales Arguments

When Ken Bradley had finished his story (see the example about the woman buying a Rex from Supreme Hardware on page 28) another of his salespeople, Rose Macauley, asked this question:

"How about the Lion Brand lawnmowers that Reggie Nollins sells? (See example, page 19.) He is very good at telling us about the features and advantages of his line, and I don't see how we can improve on his sales arguments. He really does give us the best way to sell the benefits of the Lion Brand."

Ken laughed.

"OK! Let's talk about that. Last week two men came in at different times and wanted to talk about buying big lawnmowers. They each talked to you, and you kept telling them about how that big 24-horsepower motor can pull a sulky seat with a heavy operator, even up a steep grade. Well, that's true. But who cares? Listen, Rose. One of those men was old. Yes, he likes to ride when he mows. But that isn't what he was worried about. He's the head groundskeeper for the Prenticeville Golf Club, and he has to worry about the maintenance of a machine they'll be using a lot all day, every day. You should have been telling him how easy it is to keep that machine running and the blades sharp."

"How about that other fellow—the good-looking, young one?" Rose asked.

Ken smiled. "I guess you didn't see the name on the pick-up truck he parked outside? You should have! Yes, he's young, but he has his own business, taking care of other people's lawns on contract; and he's strong and needs and wants exercise. So he isn't going to ride behind the mower; he'll walk and maybe even push. He's interested in saving gas, in getting the mower on and off his pickup, in quick, reliable service, and in replacement parts.

"Now, Reggie Nollins gives a good sales talk on the different benefits of that same big Lion Brand machine, which fit both those kinds of requirements exactly; and you could have individualized your selling for each of those men by using those good standard sales arguments he gave you—but also by personalizing them, using the right ones to fit what each men wants.

"So, the idea is this. Personalize your selling, but use standardized sales arguments when they fit the interests of the individual prospect."

Remember: To sell the benefits effectively, you may want to draw upon the standardized sales arguments for the detailed,authoritative information you need. But you may do a better job of communicating if you put the standardized sales arguments into your own language, carefully adapted—personalized—to emphasize the particular values that you know are of special interest to the prospect.

After all, the standard language in the manufacturer's brochures, for instance, is meant for everyone. That means it can't do the job of selling as well as competent communication that is shaped precisely for one particular selling situation, that matches the needs and values of one active prospect with whom you have established a relationship.

Many successful salespeople individualize all their selling, and hand out brochures and bulletins, with relevant "official selling language," only to support and reinforce what they say.

Make the best use of the standard sales arguments available to you. But if you want maximum Motivational Selling Leverage, use your *Relationship*; sell the right *Benefits* in a way that will have maximum selling effect, and let the standard selling arguments come into your *Communication* only when you feel they will add Force to what you say.

When to "Sell the Sizzle" and When to "Sell the Steak"

People have different ideas about benefits, and some make their buying decisions for reasons that others would reject as illogical or even silly. Many buying decisions are made because someone else has made a similar purchase. The psychological factors behind buyer motivations are exploited by advertisers and often very effectively.

The distinct characteristic of such advertisements is the *endorsement* of the product or service. This may include the endorsement of specific benefits, as when a movie star recites the advantages of owning a certain make of car, drinking a particular brand of coffee, wearing a particular designer's jeans, or using a certain manufacturer's cosmetics.

The face-to-face salesperson can follow the same lead. ("I sold a suit just like this to the president of the Imperial Bank yesterday." "The conductor of the Brooklyn Orchestra bought one of these hi-fi outfits last week." "Tex Gurgle [a leading country-and-western singer] gave a car like this to his girl-friend, Dixie Blast [a rising bluegrass warbler] for her birthday.") Such statements may emphasize benefits, but even when they do not, they have at least two effects that may help the sale. They imply that some well-known person, presumably in a position to make an informed choice, has perceived superior benefits in the product offered, and they provide a basis—however tenuous—for some degree of identification with a celebrity. ("These boots were made for me by the same guy that makes 'em for the President!")

Clever restaurateurs know that people often order dishes like those being served at nearby tables—especially when the people being served look like they know what they are doing. In some restaurants the management has catered to such second-hand tastes by offering spectacular service of special items, particularly of the *flambe* variety, where the food is brought to the table blazing in burning cognac (or denatured alcohol). Sometimes, to emphasize the flaming entree or dessert, the lights are turned off. And some diners order such special items, at very special prices, not to gratify their tastes, but out of vanity or a desire to be conspicuous. No doubt some patrons order champagne for similar reasons: they are paying for the attention-attracting benefit of the popping cork.

People in stores of all kinds, from high-fashion boutiques to supermarkets, are often influenced by what they see others buy. The alert salesperson will detect the interest of the prospect in such nonintrinsic benefits and find ways to use such insights in his or her selling.

Motivational Selling Leverage provides three ways selling effectiveness can be increased by catering to such nonfunctional values, when these are important to the prospect:

1. The salesperson's *Relationship* with the prospect can be favorably enhanced by some connection with a celebrity; the connection may be direct, indirect, or simply by analogy.

2. The salesperson's *Communication* may gain added force and appeal by appropriate reference to some well-regarded individuals.

3. The *Benefits* may be more convincingly sold, or persuasively implied or suggested, when they are perceived to have had decisive appeal to an identified personage.

Selling of this nature should be recognized as indirect and seldom an adequate substitute for direct selling. It may be compared to selling a steak by its "sizzle."

A popular book on selling originated the slogan: "Sell the sizzle instead of the steak." The idea was that the "sizzle" is a benefit that will appeal to many people. However, restaurants "sell" their steaks by stressing different benefits in their advertising and promotion.

Some restaurants emphasize the *quality* of their meat (Prime, New York cut, Kansas City cut, etc.). Others stress the *size* of their steaks (16-ounce sirloin, 8-ounce boneless tenderloin). Others use adjectives to suggest attractive characteristics (juicy, tender, flavor-filled, aged). Still others stress the bargain prices of their steaks.

But all the people who are motivated to order steaks, whether for their quality, size, desirable characteristics, or low price, expect them to be served as ordered (rare, medium, medium rare, etc.) and to have them served hot, just off the broiler.

So, why "sell the sizzle"? Maybe because the steaks are not of high quality, large size, or "very good," and are being sold in a restaurant where customers do not order steak very often. The mental picture of a sizzling steak would be especially attractive to such customers.

So, when you select a restaurant and order a steak—whatever the "benefits" you have in mind—don't just "buy the sizzle" unless that's what you want most!

Of course, you order a steak only when you want to eat; and when you are not hungry you are simply not in the market for a meal. If you are hungry, and you walk into a restaurant and sit at a table without having made up your mind just what you want to eat, you look at the menu. Then, unless something happens to make you get up and walk out, you are going to buy *something*.

What you buy will depend on the benefits that you value; and that you associate with something you see on the bill-of-fare, or something the waiter recommends, or something you see being served to someone else. Those prospective benefits can make you drool, if you value them enough. And the hungrier you are, the more value they will seem to have to fill your need.

The Three Exciting Elements of Selling Leverage in Action

Understanding the Great Advantage of Selling as a Whole Salesperson

There are at least two good reasons why salespeople should understand themselves well. First: It is universally true that anyone can operate best when they know and understand exactly what they have to work with in the way of tools, equipment, resources, etc. The basic equipment of all salespeople is, of course, themselves. The better they know and understand what sort of persons they are, what assets and liabilities and they have not only as salespeople, but also as people—the better they will be able to exploit their strengths and minimize their weaknesses.

It is often said of some salespeople that they "can sell only one way." They can be effective when the situation happens to fit their particular style, but they are at a loss when their style does not fit the situation because they are not aware of their "equipment," and so cannot adapt to the selling situation.

The second reason why salespeople need to have a reliable picture of themselves is that effective selling means establishing and controlling (or at least influencing) the *Relationship* with the prospect. To be able to do this, salespersons must not only have an understanding of the prospect (as discussed in Chapter 3) but they must also *see themselves in relation to the prospect.*

This includes having a reasonably accurate idea of how they look to their prospects. If the salesperson is to have the sort of influence on the prospect that they need to have, their "image" must be appropriate. This image need not be the same for every prospect, and it need not be entirely favorable. It need only be appropriate to each prospect.

Many salespersons believe that it is necessary to be liked—to establish a friendly basis by telling jokes, discussing sports, flattering the prospect, or showing interest in his or her family, hobbies, or health, etc. It is true that such elements can be an asset within an overall relationship, and that some salespeople can parlay this kind of easy cajolerie into repeat orders. But this can be done only in some situations, with some prospects.

Prospects are often busy and have no time to waste. They appreciate it when a sales call is "all business." In addition, many potential buyers are suspicious of salespeoples' camaraderie, and they may find it offensive, or it may make them feel uneasy or even insecure. Such buyers feel more comfortable with the salesperson who stays with a straightforward interview.

In view of such considerations, you can readily see the need to adapt appropriately to different prospects. If you are to do this successfully, you must not only understand them—you must also understand yourself.

Salespersons differ tremendously, and each one tends to sell in his or her own way. Most of them could extend and broaden the effectiveness of their own way of selling if they would introduce a little system into the way they apply it and also learn how to pick situations where that way is most likely to be effective.

Example: Do Better by Knowing What You Do Best

Betty Grimes is a rather methodical, persistent salesperson, who does pretty well by making a lot of calls and collecting a fair number of small to medium-size orders. One day she is greatly impressed because one of her fellow-salespeople, Ron Newcomb, has booked a very big order—equal to what Betty might book in weeks of selling. So Betty makes up her mind to go after some big orders.

But these big orders must be secured by working on a higher level of buying decision than Betty is used to; they are the result of months of promoting with department heads and vice-presidents, and they involve modifications of product, technical considerations, special credit, price, payment and delivery arrangements, and other factors that Betty is not well equipped to handle. So she wastes a lot of time trying. Her regular sales fall off, and she never does get a big order.

Betty failed to understand herself. If she had, she would have realized that, to succeed with the big orders, she would have had to change her way of selling, and so, herself. She would have had to learn considerably more, and she would have had to develop some new know-how about prospects, and even some new personal characteristics. If she had understood herself better, she could have recognized the need for this self-development, and she could have decided to bring about these changes in herself—or stick to her own proven path.

Salespeople need to adapt effectively to each prospect. Ideally, the salesperson should be thinking: "This prospect is *this* kind of person; I am *this* kind of salesperson. How, then, can I best use what I am, and what I have, in *this* situation, toward getting *this* person to buy?"

There can be no intelligent selling strategy without an adequate realization of the major personal factors, and the most skillful tactics are wasted unless they are adapted to these factors.

How to be a Whole Salesperson

Thousands of books have been written on how to understand oneself, and philosophers and religious leaders have tried to illumine this subject through the ages. No claim is made that the system offered in this book is the long-sought answer to this basic problem of mankind. But those who make a serious effort to apply it to themselves will find it not only professionally useful, but also personally enlightening.

In particular, the system of self-evaluation outlined in this chapter can help you to understand important factors in the *Relationship* between yourself and the prospect.

To begin with, in considering the "Whole Salesperson," it is emphasized that, in selling, *all* of you is important. But it is impossible to consider the whole person at one time, so we have to divide the subject in some way in order to handle it. For our purposes, the most appropriate and useful way to divide it is into four basic parts.

So to start, take a central point, divide the space around it into four parts (as shown in Diagram 3-1), number the spaces I, II, III, and IV, and label each as in the diagram. Then, in the appropriate space, jot down a self-description as you go through the following pages.

This is the frame for a "picture" of *you*, the Whole Salesperson.

Be thoughtful and honest about this, because if you are not, you will be making a picture that is not *you* and that cannot help you sell.

Understanding the Basic You and Weighing Your Background Knowledge

Part I: The Basic You

You are born with many inherited tendencies and potentials. In the earliest part of your life a great deal of your personality was formed from the effects of your childhood experience on your hereditary base. This is the basic *you*—the psychological skeleton, or core, that determines much of the way you are, and the way you behave. This is the part of you that is most permanent and unchanging, and which is hardest to change. This is the you

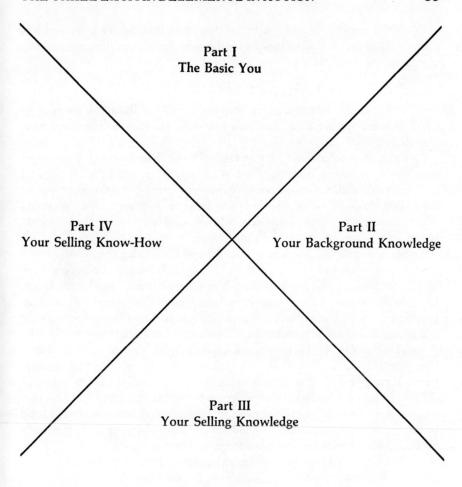

Part I
The Basic You

Part IV
Your Selling Know-How

Part II
Your Background Knowledge

Part III
Your Selling Knowledge

Diagram 3-1
THE WHOLE SALESPERSON

that usually underlies whatever you want or feel or do. This is what you write into Part I.

You should also list in Part I the major "fixed assets" you have as an individual, such as your general educational and family background and important formative experiences. You can also list any special knowledge or ability, hobby or skill, interest or activity that is important to you, but which is *not* related to your work. For instance, if you are an amateur chef, and you do *not* sell food, cooking equipment, or anything else that is related to your hobby, that hobby is listed in Part I.

Think about this basic you. This is what you "carry" with you wherever you go, and whatever you do. It has a great deal to do with how everything looks or seems to you. Everything you say and every decision you make is affected and influenced by the basic you. Everyone you come in contact with will have a chance to see some of that basic you. So the basic you has a major effect on your *Relations* with others, including your prospects, and, of course, on your selling.

Part II: Your Background Knowledge

This includes information of ongoing relevance about the industry in which you are involved: its processes, practices, markets, competition, people, etc.

Every product and service that you sell has a "background." This ranges from the materials, technology, and skills that enter into production, and the factors that affect design, quality, supply, pricing, marketing, etc., to the uses and applications, the basis for value to customers, the variations in purchasing and demand, the competition, and the newest developments in the supplying industries and the market.

No one can have "complete" background knowledge of *any* industry—there is too much for any one person to know. But some salespeople have very little background knowledge, while others have a broad knowledge. In some situations, background knowledge may be unnecessary; in other situations it may be very helpful—if only to put you on a sound footing with a prospect. For some prospects, such knowledge is essential to make the sale.

Think about the background knowledge you have of your industry. You probably have more than you realize. What about previous employment? Have you studied subjects which shed light on any part of the industry? Do you have a hobby, special experience, or military training that provides some related knowledge? (If you are an amateur chef and you *do* sell food or kitchen equipment, this is the place to list that hobby, or any other hobby that adds to background knowledge of your industry.)

If you have worked for a different employer in the same field, you have some background knowledge that others do not have. If you have visited plants, have seen special applications, or know important figures in the industry, list that in Part II of your diagram. And if you take special plant tours, make inspections, take related courses, or sit in on seminars or training programs that add to your background knowledge, list these, too.

Do not list anything in Part II that relates directly to anything you are selling, how you are to sell it, or to any individual customer or prospect you know. All of that belongs in Part III.

Evaluating Your Selling Knowledge and Selling Know-How

Part III: Your Selling Knowledge

Selling knowledge is the term applied to what you learn from your organization through such sources as training, memos, bulletins, prospect lists, instructions and directives from management and data on territories. Such forms of communication constitute one major source of selling information.

There is also the information that you pick up while selling or making sales calls—data, leads, tips, hints, impressions, insights and news about the industry, market, and competition. All this information makes up the other major source of selling knowledge.

It includes or relates to items in which prospects are or may be interested; the person or persons dealt with; the nature and details of the prospect's general purchasing patterns, such as specifications, price and delivery data; credit; and similar specifics. Here you would include all those matters related to specific prospects or actual customers.

Most salespeople pick up selling knowledge from their own company, from the training they receive, and from direct sales contacts. But other sources may also be very useful, or even necessary, such as business publications and trade journals, other salespersons (even competitors), prospects, receptionists and secretaries, and the daily newspaper.

Part IV: Your Selling Know-How

Since most salespersons have or can acquire similar sources of information, the big difference among them is, usually, not only in *having* or not having a particular item of knowledge that can swing the balance their way, but also in knowing just *how*—or the best way—to use that knowledge. And this you can learn, most of the time, only from the prospect. The prospect will seldom tell you his or her thoughts directly. You must learn for yourself through interaction with the prospect.

That is one of the most important ways in which conversation leads to transaction. The more you know about yourself (Part I), your background (Part II), and the handling of prospects (Part III), the more likely you will be to have the know-how about *what* to say to sell the prospect.

The Know-How of selling lies in making the best use of your personality (I), your background knowledge (II), and your selling knowledge (III) to sell *this* prospect. That means, applying what you are and what you have to use as effectively as possible in each contact with a prospect.

This Know-How is usually applied in the face-to-face selling conversation; though it may also be applied in letters, or telephone calls, or any other kind of communication. But most of the time, the successful sale is based on information largely derived from the prospect him- or herself. This should be easiest to manage—and the results should be most valuable—in the course of a face-to-face session.

This does not mean that all the Know-How is formulated and worked out at such times. Thoughtful consideration after a meeting of what actually took place, and why, and what it signifies and what to do about it; a study of your notes about this prospect; and careful planning before the next meeting are all useful. The salesperson who likes to improvise—to "play it by ear"—may have a lot of conversational know-how, but in the long run the salespersons who "do their homework" are more likely to get the highest marks.

Basically, Know-How helps you to utilize effectively *all* that you are—
the *whole* salesperson.

In the other sections of this chapter we will discuss these four elements
of the Whole Salesperson in greater detail and indicate how they can best
be utilized in selling to the Whole Prospect. In other parts of this book we
talk about putting it all together, to produce successful professional selling,
with Motivational Selling Leverage.

Why Two People Have Six Personalities and What This Means in Selling

When any two people are talking together, how many "persons" (or
personalities) are present? Six, according to Oliver Wendell Holmes, in his
Autocrat at the Breakfast Table.

By applying his idea to selling, we see that a salesperson and a prospect can be "seen" as six different personalities.

1. The Whole Salesperson as he or she really is.

2. The Whole Prospect as he or she really is.

3. The salesperson as the prospect sees him or her.

4. The prospect as the salesperson sees him or her.

5. The salesperson as he or she sees him- or herself.

6. The prospect as he or she sees him- or herself.

What all this means is that, instead of #1 selling to #2, a *team* of #1,
#3, and #5 is trying to sell to a *team* of #2, #4, and #6.

Like any other team, of course, #1, #3, and #5 have a better chance
if they are organized, have practiced, and if they work well together. For
this to happen, the salesperson must see himself realistically and must understand his basic self. It also means the salesperson must present an "image"
to the prospect that has a sound working relationship with the "image" the
salesperson has of himself.

But it also means that the salesperson needs to be aware of a great deal
about the prospect, including any important differences between #2 and #4.
The salesperson should also have a good idea of where #6 ties into, or differs from, these.

It's a very good idea to develop a diagram, as much like Diagram 3-1
as possible, for your Whole Prospect. That should help you to understand
your prospect, and therefore to sell him or her far more successfully.

In addition to the personalities themselves, there are likely to be other
elements in the meeting which can be decisive. These may include past
relationships, preconceptions and prejudices, and such considerations as

value, price, quality, quantity, need, competition, policies, habits, availability, delivery, and credit. Of course, all or most of these may be quite outside the salesperson's control.

But the salesperson should be able to control the relations between #1, #3, and #5; and understand as much as possible about the relations between #2, #4, and #6. The salesperson who does this can greatly increase the probbility that #1 will succeed in selling to #2 (or #3 to #6).

Now, relate all this with yourself as a Whole Salesperson. You can see that each of the four parts of you—(Part I) the basic you, (Part II) your background, (Part III) your selling knowledge, and (Part IV) your selling know-how—can help a lot to get your "3-person team" organized, coordinated, and working well.

#1. All four of the parts of your Whole Salesperson come into #1, you, the salesperson, as you really are.

#3. Some of your Part I and Part II will enter #3, as the prospect sees you; but if you make the sale, it will probably be because of your Parts III and IV.

#5. If #5, as you see yourself, is very different from #3, as the prospect sees you, you may not make the sale.

Remember that there are also four Parts to the Whole Prospect, just as there are in the Whole Salesperson.

#4. What you see and hear may be mostly from his or her Parts III and IV, but you had better be able to learn from the prospect's Part II, and also something about the prospect's Part I—so there won't be too much difference between #2, the prospect as he really is, and #4, the prospect as you see him.

#6. You need to use all your Part III and Part IV to make sure that you treat the prospect in a way that fits his or her own self-image.

Remember, when you are selling, that all six of these "personalities" are involved. Remember, too, that three of you are selling to three of "them," all at one time, in one Whole Prospect. So be sure to keep your own three personalities in shape for good teamwork.

What Is a "Prospect"?

Prospect is a word that salespeople, sales managers, and marketing and advertising people use loosely. By and large, they usually mean a person who *may* become a customer. When you are selling, each person you are dealing with is a Whole Person; but it can be harmfully deceptive to your selling to consider any Whole Person as *the* prospect.

To explore this matter and to arrive at a sound working understanding of the word *prospect*, let us look at a few illustrative situations, beginning with one that is familiar and uncomplicated.

Example: The Stroller as a Prospect

From his mobile refrigerator, Tony Bindo sells Frozen Ecstasies on a street corner. The confections are bought by passersby and by the neighborhood children. Many of these are regular customers. But what is a "prospect" to Tony? *Any* passerby? *Any* child? Constantly ringing a bell and calling out the names and flavors of his tasty wares, Tony treats all passersby and children as prospects. But are they?

Some passersby wouldn't buy *anything* from a street vendor; some are on diets; others have tried Tony's treats and won't try them again; some prefer the "Chilled Delight" offered on the next corner; and some just aren't in the mood.

Some of the children have no cash; others have, but are saving it for other indulgences; some have been admonished or forbidden by their parents; and some are in too much of a hurry.

Were any of these passersby and children actually prospects? How many of them could a more effective salesperson have turned into customers?

Young Timmy Bowman comes up with just enough change to buy two Frozen Ecstasies, one for himself and the other for his younger sister. His mother, looking out from a window above, has given him the money, after prolonged pleas. Was Timmy a prospect? Was his mother?

The manufacturer of Frozen Ecstasies, a division of a large subsidiary of a major conglomerate, advertises Frozen Ecstasies on national television, and the local distributor promotes it on local TV and radio. At what stage of awareness do watchers or listeners become prospects?

Tony is not very sophisticated about selling, and knows almost nothing about the broader aspects of marketing. But he is making a living. To him, almost anyone in sight is a prospect; those out of sight are not. Now let us look at a more elaborate situation.

Example: When Is a Prospect Not a Prospect?

Ed Derwinski heads his own insurance agency, with eight salespeople out selling for him, and he is constantly striving to provide them with prospects.

Ed does this mainly by his own advertising, by buying lists, and through responses to the local advertising of the national companies he represents.

Edith Neff, one of Ed's salespeople, is mature, thoughtful, and extremely systematic. One day she leaves a note on Ed's desk, telling him she wants to see him after hours. Promptly at closing time she is at his desk.

"Ed," she begins, "I have kept a running record for six months now of my experience with different sources of prospects. During this period, I made a total of 1,108 contacts. Most were just one telephone call. Some were one face-to-face meeting. From all these contacts, I had a total of 78 sales. But what I want to talk to you about is the difference in the sources of prospects.

"You gave me 279 names from returns to our own advertising. I was able to see only 53 of them, and I sold 14; that's 5 percent sold. You gave me 521 names from lists you bought. I was able to see only 26 of them, and I sold 6; that's 1 percent. You gave me 342 names from returns to company advertising. I was able to see only 69 of them, and I sold 16; that's almost 5 percent. Now, that's a total of 1,142 names that you gave me, supposed to be prospects. I was able to see only 148 of them, and I sold 36, 24 percent, which is only 3 percent of the total number of prospects.

"But—lucky for me—I have three other sources of prospects: referrals from those I have already sold; referrals through friends and other contacts of my own; and my own prospecting—such as in organizations I have joined or have managed to get to in one way or another.

"I had 43 referrals from my customers; saw all but one of them, and sold 21; that's 49 percent. I had 38 names from friends and personal contacts; saw all of them, and sold 12; that's 32 percent. I developed 89 prospects* on my own; saw 71 of them, and sold 9; that's 10 percent. Altogether, I contacted 170 prospects from sources other than those you gave me; was able to see 151 of them, and sold 42, which is 25 percent.

"During those six months, I figure I spent more than three quarters of my time, trying to follow through on your sources of prospects, and I made less than half of my sales from those sources. Was that worthwhile? I was able to make most of my sales in less than one-quarter of my time by doing my own prospecting."

Ed was thoughtful.

"There's a good lesson in this for all of us," he finally said. "What *is* a prospect? Is it just any name on a list that somebody thinks may be a prospect? Is it somebody you can't even get in to see?"

"Yes, Ed," Edith agreed, "that's exactly my point. Is it somebody who may be ready to buy, but already has an agent, a broker, a cousin, or a friend?"

"Or who has an insurance company they prefer, which isn't one we represent?" said Ed.

"Or who is only checking out competitive rates before renewing coverages they already have with somebody else?" added Edith.

"I've got a lot to think about, Edith," Ed finally acknowledged. "Let's all have a conference about prospects and prospecting, and, Edith, you start it out with what you told me."

---

*Note: In this book, the term *prospect* is used broadly and applies to any person the salesperson may be dealing with in hope of a sale.

How to Be a Whole Salesperson
to the Whole Prospect

Every person is a *whole* person. But when we are in contact with another person, we tend to see only a small part of that person, usually the "side" which is noticeably active in the particular role they are involved in at the time. There are other times when that "same" person plays other roles; then they seem to be very different, because they are intent on other matters, moved by other values, following other interests, reacting to different conditions, and trying to satisfy other needs.

We all know that people appear differently as they respond to different situations. The police officer who stops you in an authoritative way for a traffic violation probably doesn't act that way with his wife and children. The young store clerk who answers curtly when you ask her a question doesn't behave that way on a date. The carpenter who casually tells you how long you'll have to wait to get a job done doesn't talk that way to the plumber when he wants a leak fixed in a bathroom of his own home.

The same principle is true for salespeople and prospects. The better you understand this principle, the better you'll sell. That side of a person you see at any given moment is like the tip of an iceberg; there's so much more you don't see which may be more important.

Of course, the same thing goes for the other person—the prospect—looking at you. What side of you do they see? Is it the best side? Is it the side that will do the most good to make the sale?

You know that there is a great deal more to you than your role as a salesperson. If you let the prospect see you, and think of you, in only that one role, you are giving up your chance to let the prospect perceive the rest of you. Only when they see more can you begin to establish a *Relationship* that can make a lot of difference in whether or not you are successful in your selling.

Most salespersons have their own "selling personality"—the way they talk and act when they are selling. This tends to become rather stereotyped. They tend to treat every prospect the same way; they give the same sales talk to everyone.

Such behavior usually changes somewhat when the *Relationship* with a prospect develops. For it is almost impossible not to adjust, at least a little, to what other persons say and do.

But then the question is, what changes should we make to adapt to the situation effectively?

Can you do a better job of selling by keeping the relationship on a "pure" salesperson/prospect basis? Or can you do better if you develop a fuller relationship?

Bear in mind that your prospect or customer is a Whole Person; there is considerably more to him or her than is showing at any given moment;

and don't forget that you are also a Whole Person, not only a salesperson. Don't let the interaction between you and the prospect be limited to a narrow salesperson–prospect channel. Be sure that the relationship includes some contact between the two Whole Persons involved, and that the interests and values between you include more than your desire to sell and his or her possible decision to buy.

A basic approach toward building a fuller *Relationship* involves finding and sharing a common interest apart from whatever it is you want to sell and he or she might buy. Entertaining prospects should help you to get to know them better; but you can do a great deal more to create or cement the right kind of *Relationship* when you know the prospects' interests, and you can do even more to build good *Relationships* when you truly share those interests.

Shared interests can range from talking about football or baseball to watching games together; from discussing hobbies to bowling or playing bridge together; from "rapping" on music, movies, or the theater to spending evenings together in such favored entertainments; from asking about the health of the prospect's spouse and children to arranging joint family outings. There are many thoughtful, constructive ways for a salesperson to build a worthwhile personal *Relationship* with a prospect or customer that leads to, parallels, and strengthens a business *Relationship*.

All this is particularly important in a continuing relationship, when you will be seeing the customer from time to time or on a regular basis. But it also applies to a single-contact situation, such as door-to-door selling. For instance, an effective "ploy" used by people who sell magazine subscriptions door to door is that they are "working their way through college." They have found that this identification (which may or may not be true) causes some prospects to perceive them, not as mere peddlers, but as "real people," and this has a more favorable effect on the buying decision.

The Importance of Treating Each Prospect as a Whole Person

When you are approached by a person who is trying to sell you something, you get certain impressions. One of the impressions you may get is that you are listening to a "parrot," simply mouthing standard sales talk, spouting memorized quotes from the company's sales manual. What the salesperson says is not responsive to what you say. It is almost like pressing a button or dialing and getting a pre-recorded message that was left—not for you—but for anyone who pressed the same button or dialed the same number.

What they say may tell you what you want to know, but it doesn't inspire confidence. That is because you don't get the feeling that the salesperson knows what he is talking about; he is simply repeating what he has been told to say. As long as such a situation continues, you can't help but think of the salesperson as *only* that—a salesperson who is trying to sell you something; and, even if the product or service is something you might like to have, you would probably prefer to buy it from somebody else.

When salespeople like that are trying to sell to you in that way, you are not getting the picture of a *whole* person. A whole person is there, but that is *not* what you "see." You don't see a whole person because he is showing you only a small part (and not the best part) of him- or herself.

Don't be like that. Don't try to sell that way.

You are a whole person—so act like one!

It's easy. Be natural. Be yourself. Let your whole self take over—not only your "salesperson self." Use the information you have, but don't simply quote from the company's blurbs.

LISTEN to the prospect carefully, and be as responsive as you can to what the prospect says. Give him or her plenty of opportunity to react to what you say—to ask questions, comment, object, etc.

Try to figure out what the prospect is thinking, what he is trying to communicate to you, and *why* (what's behind it). Then make what you say as responsive to that as possible.

It will not take long for the prospect to realize that he is talking with a *whole* person—an intelligent, responsive, understanding person who is *listening carefully and with interest*, who is helpfully informative, and who happens to be offering a product or service that's beginning to sound interesting!

To you, of course, he is important as a prospective customer; but to himself, his importance is that of a *whole* person. That is why, if you want to make your *Relationship* with the prospect into a factor for motivation to buy from you, you must always remember that each prospect is a *Whole Person*. If you bear that fundamental truth in mind, and act on it, you will be more likely to establish a *Relationship* in which the prospect becomes a customer.

Every person has different relationships with other people. Some people are suspicious, "cold," and very formal in their business relationships. Others are friendly, warm, and outgoing, sincerely and naturally pleasant and receptive—and often helpful—even in business relationships.

Every person acts out many different roles in his or her different relationships. The person who enjoys the role of loving father or mother to his or her children may not enjoy, but may still assume, the role of tough, exacting, cold-blooded purchasing agent, buyer, or prospect of any other kind. But that may make a Whole Person to Whole Person relationship even more important!

Remember that it may take a lot of doing to get that final "yes!" Your goal is to make that sale; but you may have to reach a few necessary or appropriate subgoals on the way. And to reach these subgoals, of course, you have to know what they are or should be. (Subgoals are more fully discussed in Chapters 4 and 5.)

Well, if you have the right kind of relationship with the prospect, he or she is much more likely to put you on the track of those subgoals; and if the prospect tells you what they are, you may be on your way to that sale. If the prospect just says "No!" you may never understand what those subgoals should have been.

Understanding the Collective Prospect

The questions raised by Edith and Ed after she reported her six-month experience, on page 45, emphasize the problems about the word *prospect*, and what it should mean. But there is another complication of great importance in many selling situations, and that is the *Collective Prospect*.

Example: The Collective Prospect

Toby Dembitz sells a line of electronic measuring instruments and other devices for Graduate Equipment Company. He is making his first call at the new plant of Stellar Dynamics, which his sales manager has assured him is a very hot prospect for their products. He has just introduced himself to the purchasing agent, Angus McKenna, who is leafing through the technical literature Toby has placed before him.

"Well, Mr. Dembitz, I'm glad you came by," McKenna was saying. "We know your company. I believe we are using some of your equipment in our other plants, and there is a good chance we will be doing business together. So let me explain how we proceed.

"Your products are highly technical and have many highly technical applications. You will have to discuss them with people who have the qualifications to evaluate them for our purposes. I should think that would include the director of our laboratory, probably some of the specialized people who report to him, the Manager of Quality Assurance, and probably the chairman of our Committee on Standards. Then there's the Engineering Department, and Production Control, and maybe Maintenance, Technical Services, and possibly, Customer Relations. Any purchase might have to be approved by Corporate Technology at our headquarters in Poughkeepsie, and perhaps by our Committee on Instrumentation; and of course, after all that, it goes through my office for our OK on price and on competitive alternatives. You're undoubtedly familiar with this kind of situation from your experience elsewhere."

Toby later reports to his sales manager about this call: "You told me Stellar Dynamics was a hot prospect. I think you're right, but its a big outfit, with lots of people who have something to say about what the company buys. So I'm going to have quite a time finding out which people to sell and getting to see them."

"Yes, indeed, Toby," the sales manager says. "Stellar Dynamics is just another example of what I call a *Collective Prospect.*"

How does a *Collective Prospect* differ from other kinds of prospects?

Few prospects are simply one individual, because few individuals make purchases uninfluenced by others. Individuals who buy usually do so for a set of reasons. And most, if not all, of those reasons may be traceable to someone else.

A man buying a suit for himself will probably be influenced by the preferences of his absent wife, the example of a well-dressed acquaintance, the publicized modeling of a screen star, or by the advice of a friend; and probably more than one of these factors will influence his buying decision.

If his wife or a friend were present, there would be a relatively simple *Collective Prospect.* The salesperson would try to satisfy them both in order to make the sale.

An extensive and involved organizational network, such as Toby Dembitz encountered at Stellar Dynamics, represents a more complex, more formalized, and more organized *Collective Prospect.*

Example: Dealing with the Collective Prospect

Toby remembers a time, years ago, when he sold cars. It was not unusual for a whole family to appear in the showroom. Some of the family members had very definite ideas about engines, body styles, seats, radio, accessories, performance characteristics, and other features. Toby had to answer questions—some silly, but others quite sophisticated; and enter into serious discussions with the older children, and even with some outspoken boys of ten. (He realized that by doing this he was building *Relationships* that made him a favorite; that he was thus enabled to sell a number of *Benefits* he might not otherwise have dwelt upon so extensively, because he had not suspected the needs or wants they could satisfy.) And he was given the opportunity to adapt his *Communication* to the particular interests and knowledge levels of each junior, while the parents stood by appreciatively smiling. Such families were *Collective Prospects,* if anything ever was!

When you encounter a *Collective Prospect,* you must learn how to deal with each individual who is in a position to influence a sale. Each person, therefore, must be treated as an individual prospect.

Each individual in the *Collective Prospect* may be concerned about different *Benefits,* such as capacity, efficiency, adaptability, reliability, safety, durability, maintainability, weight, size, and power requirements. Furthermore, the bases of decision are often divided up among a number of individuals. Some may have a veto, others must indicate approval, no objection, no alternative, or urgent need. Still others may be responsible for weighing alternatives, competitive offerings, value, price, etc.

The salesperson must find the way through this forest and learn enough about each individual prospect to apply the most effective Motivational Selling Leverage. Doing this well the first time can prove to be a lucrative investment, as the *Collective Prospect's* needs and wants continue to grow.

How to Get a Good Look at the Whole Prospect

There are a number of ways of finding out what you need to know about the prospect, if you are to do the best job of selling that you are able to do—which means doing all that can be done to build up in the prospect the greatest possible motivation to buy from you.

What are these ways to find out what you will need to know? Here are some of the most important:

1. Ask around.
2. Do research by reading trade journals, sales records, Department of Commerce reports, and get information in trade association libraries, etc.
3. Conduct a study via telephone, letters, or personal calls of your competitors, or of the prospect's customers and competitors, etc.
4. Get the prospect to tell you.

Nine times out of ten, the easiest and best way is to get the prospect to tell you what you need to know. But you do have to motivate the prospect to tell you, and that involves creating the right *Relationship*. Then the Fulcrum begins to slide closer to the Weight and the right *Relationship* begins to get you Motivational Selling Leverage!

What can motivate the prospect to tell you what you need to know? That is really three questions:

I. Why should the prospect want to take the time and trouble to tell you anything?

II. What do you *need* to know?

III. What can motivate the prospect to tell you that? You must first give the prospect the impression that giving you information is a logical and desirable thing for him or her to do; and the prospect will feel that way if the two following conditions are met:

a. The prospect must "see" you as a "whole person" who, in turn, "sees" himself as a "whole person." This means that the prospect must feel that he or she and you are not a prospect and a salesperson in typical cliché confrontation, but two intelligent, constructively minded "Whole People."

b. The prospect must also "see" that you are reasonably objective and that you desire to work out a constructive development to a situation in which the prospect has a special interest. This means that you must appear to subordinate your own interests and accept the prospect's interests as paramount.

Once the prospect gets the idea that you are willing to contribute along lines that interest the prospect, the conditions will exist that can motivate the prospect to tell you about the situation from his point of view. You can help this process by asking questions, but the questions must be aimed at exploring the situation *the prospect* is talking about. If you try to sell at this stage, you may spoil the conditions that motivate the prospect to talk, and this will slide the Fulcrum away from the Weight, losing the Motivational Selling Leverage you had gained before.

Listen with real interest in the situation the prospect is telling you about; and ask questions to increase your understanding and comment to indicate your interest.

Once you have the story, the whole situation will have changed:

c. The prospect will have an "investment" in you; he will have told you about a situation of some importance to him, with some expectation of a helpful result.

d. Your *Relationship* with the prospect will have changed; the Fulcrum will be closer to the Weight, and you will have better Motivational Selling Leverage.

e. You will have learned what you need to know to make the sale.

Here is how Jay Lowen talks to an experienced purchasing agent who is new in his present position.

Example: The "Old-Timer"

Jay Lowen: "I've been around this circuit eleven years, and I know just about everybody on it. I should—I've seen them often enough. I know my competition, too. I'm friendly with most of them, and I pass the time of day with them in waiting rooms, on planes and trains, and in hotel lobbies. Some of them I've known for years; and now and then, we have a drink together or maybe dinner. Some of the purchasing agents have known me for years, and we get together, too—away from the office.

"Now, I'm telling you this because I think you are in a situation where you need some answers, and I'd like to be helpful. Since I know the industry pretty well, I think I could be of some help."

This kind of talk usually gets a good response from the newer buyers, who are usually glad to pick up information and ideas from people who have been in the business a long time. Jay knows how to make the most of his experience, and what the purchasing agents tell him is essentially what he needs to know.

Here is the way Irene Garber talks to the same purchasing agent that Jay Lowen spoke to.

Example: New on the Job

Irene Garber: "I've just started with my company, and I know I have a lot to learn. But my company has a great deal to offer you, and I will be calling on you regularly. I want to be as helpful to you as I can be. I've been doing a lot of studying, and I know our line and quite a bit about our competition.

"What I'd like to know is where we might come into the picture as far as meeting your needs. The better I understand what you are interested in, and the special ways your company does business, the better I can develop and facilitate the benefits you can derive from dealing with us."

This approach works well for Irene. Most of the buyers she calls on for the first time take the time to fill her in on what they look for, what they don't care about, and how they do business.

Both Jay and Irene view their prospects as Whole Persons. Beginning on that sound basis, they do not find it difficult to learn what they need to know to make sales.

We go further into the matter of getting information from the prospect when we discuss Feedback in Chapter 4.

How Selling Leverage Helps You Pinpoint Needs, Wants, and Motivations

The Two Most Important Factors in Any Selling Situation

What do you need most when you are selling?

You need to know whatever will help you to sell to a particular prospect.

Here is a way to learn what you need to know; a *system* that will help you to understand what to do, what direction to go, and how to get there. Motivational Selling Leverage will help you to know this.

If you are a stranger and lost in New York City, you would want to know where you are, so you can figure out how to get to where you want to go. If someone tells you that you are on Broadway, that helps, but you could be anywhere along the fifteen miles or so of Broadway. If you wanted to get to the United Nations, or Radio City from Broadway, you wouldn't know which way to go. You would need to know where you are on Broadway—near what crosstown street. You would need to locate yourself by the *intersection* of *two* streets.

When all you know is that you are somewhere on a line, you could be anywhere along its total length. But if you know you are where two lines cross, you can only be at that one point.

It is almost the same with selling: first you figure out the right *transaction*, or deal, for a prospect—one that would be reasonable for the prospect to make; then you have yourself on the right road. But you need to know where you are on that road—what communication will get *that* prospect to *buy*. When you have figured that, you will know (1) where you are; (2) where you want to go; and (3) how to get there. *Then* you can go about selling like a "pro." But without that, you are in the dark, guessing, floundering, and reacting blindly.

Some salespeople never get beyond that confused kind of selling. Some of them are clever enough and have been around long enough to do well. But they are playing a game; they are not running a business. They could do considerably better if they backed up their skills with solid know-how on what is the best "pitch" in a particular situation. That makes the difference between the talented amateur and the successful "pro." Know-how moves you into a different league.

The system you should use is based on the four primary elements that make up any selling situation:

The Agreement: a deal or a transaction involving an exchange of payment for a product or service.

The Talk: the *Communication* which is intended to lead to the Agreement.

The Whole Prospect: the individual who is to be led into the Agreement.

The Whole Salesperson: the individual who is to lead the prospect into the Agreement.

The system is like "a navigational fix," which is the way navigators on ships or planes find their way by locating themselves through "fixing" their positions.

They can do this with great accuracy by using a sextant to sight stars (with exact timing) and to measure the angle of each star above the horizon.

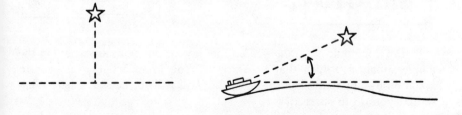

Each star-sight gives the navigator a "line-of-position." But this line-of-position runs across the world because, at that moment, the angle of that star above the horizon is the same from all points on that line. So when you have your line-of-position, you know what line you are on, but you can be any place on it.

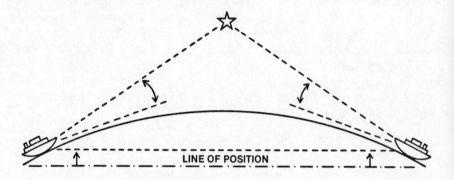

LINE OF POSITION

Now, as a salesperson, you begin by knowing what you have to sell, its price and related information. Then you look at a prospect—a person who you hope will buy from you. And you "sight" from there.

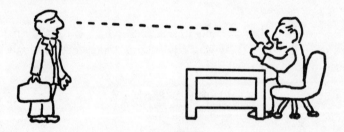

There is your first star. You sight that and measure the "angle," and that gives you your first "line-of-position," which is the Agreement that it is possible and desirable to make with *this* prospect.

WHAT YOU WILL SELL

LINE OF POSITION [the DEAL]

WHAT HE WILL BUY

But you could be *anywhere* on that line-of-position; anywhere in the *whole* situation, which that line crosses. You know what you want to accomplish—and that is half the battle. But *how* will you accomplish it? What should you do to succeed?

What you need now is another line-of-position, a line that *crosses* the first one. Then you can be at only *one* place—*where those two lines cross.* That intersection is called a *"navigational fix"* and it tells you where you are, so you know exactly which way to go to get to where you want to be.

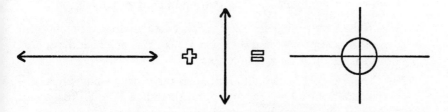

How do you get this second line-of-position? You start from knowing about yourself as a Whole Salesperson, and you sight toward the person you are trying to sell as a Whole Prospect. You measure this "angle," and you come up with your second line-of-position. This should tell you what benefits to sell and how best to sell them, which is your cue to the right *Communication*—the interchange between you and the prospect that has the greatest likelihood of making the sale. This *Communication* is the right one for *this* selling situation.

T
R
A
N
S
COMMUNICATION
C
T
I
O
N

Where the right Transaction meets the right Communication is where you should be!

Consider for a moment what this simple, basically correct system involves.

1a: You are a salesperson. You have something to sell. You are there to sell it. If you aim at the *right* target, you *can* sell it. If you aim at anything else, you probably cannot.

1b: You want to sell it to *this* person. He is a possible buyer. Under *some conditions* this prospect will buy.

1c: The only thing you can sell the prospect is the Transaction that is possible; the Deal that the prospect will accept. This potential Agreement is a primary factor between you and the prospect, which you need to know if you are to make a·sale.

How do you go about learning that and acting effectively on it?

2a: You are different from other people and, therefore, different from other salespeople; and there is a Whole You of which the "pure" salesperson is only a small part.

2b: The prospect is also different from other people and, thus, different from other prospects; and there is a Whole Prospect of which the "pure" prospect is only a small part.

2c: You and the prospect relate to one another the way people ordinarily do, by communicating.

2d: As a unique person, you communicate in certain characteristic ways. Some of these characteristic ways will be better than others for establishing or developing the *Relationship* you need with this particular prospect in order to make the sale.

2e: The *best* way for you to get an agreement with this Whole Prospect is by using the *Right Communication*.

So it is up to you to be where the *Communication* and the Agreement, or Deal, meet. This system will help you get there.

Understanding the Nature of the Selling Situation

What is involved in the "selling" situation? What are its principal components, and how do they affect the selling process?

To begin with, let us define the term *selling situation*. The term includes:

1. People: Usually only two individuals, the salesperson and the prospect, but sometimes more are present within the environment where the salesperson is making a selling effort.

2. Physical environment: The office, room, factory, warehouse, restaurant, car, plane, train, street-corner, etc., where the salesperson and the prospect meet.

3. Values, constraints, and influences: Those factors which may affect the utterances, decisions, or other behavior of the individuals present; and especially the degrees of interest, or the positive or negative attitudes of the prospect toward the salesperson, or toward whatever the salesperson says, does, or is trying to sell.

Your sales success depends on your understanding the significant features of the situations in which you are trying to make sales.

Every individual has different characteristics, and every environment has different characteristics. Therefore, every selling situation has so many different characteristics and combinations of characteristics that it is ridiculously inadequate to say that "every situation is different."

This inevitability of difference is as true of selling situations as it is of other kinds of situations, and the more fully you understand this, and act upon that understanding, the more effective a salesperson you will be.

The only characteristic that all selling situations have in common is the salesperson's desire to sell, and even that varies greatly among salespeople.

Even when the same salesperson is involved in different selling situations, there seldom are common characteristics because that salesperson usually cannot act in the same way in different situations. If the salesperson is so rigid that he or she does not adapt to the differences in situations, he or she will find that although the reactions will differ from situation to situation, the unsuccessful results will probably remain constant.

Since there are many ways in which selling situations differ and since the salesperson cannot possibly know and adapt to all of them, it is necessary to focus on those factors which are likely to have the most important effects on the selling process. Usually, of course, the most important identifiable factor is one person—the prospect. (When more than one person is involved, the situation becomes more complex, and we need to understand something about the relations among these people, and the relation of each of them to the buying decision. (See the Collective Prospect, page 49.)

But prospects also operate within their own situations, which have significant, and often controlling, effects. To the extent that they influence the buying decision, they must also be part of the selling situation.

Remember that "six personalities" are involved in the selling situation (see pages 42-43). When the salesperson has no control over the situation except by what he or she says or does, it becomes essential, not only to be aware of the "three personalities" of the prospect, but also to be aware of those factors in the situation which affect those personalities.

To help you understand the importance of factors which are outside the selling environment, consider this example:

Example: Getting the Prospect's Attention

Dwayne Nabors sells a line of hardware to distributors and to chains of retail stores. He has an appointment with Zeb Borchard, a buyer for a chain of department stores with large hardware departments. Zeb's chain has been a large volume customer. Dwayne wants to tell Zeb about a major special promotion his firm is planning, which should move a lot of merchandise. Dwayne is counting on Zeb to cooperate strongly in the promotion and has flown in from his home base for this meeting.

When he walks into Zeb's office, he finds Zeb rather unresponsive, and when he tries to start the usual give and take, the conversation falls flat.

Dwayne, somewhat disconcerted, starts his account of the promotion, detailing the ways retailers would participate in the promotional displays, special discounts, cooperative advertising, etc. Zeb mumbles an occasional monosyllable, as if to signify, "Yes, I understand—OK—what else?" Dwayne feels he is being hurried through his story, but finishes and leaves. He is somewhat miffed at Zeb's unusual behavior, but goes away believing that all is well and that Zeb will handle the promotion in his chain.

But, much to Dwayne's dismay, Zeb's chain does not participate.

Dwayne didn't know that Zeb had been looking forward to moving up, filling a higher position in the chain's organization, which had recently become vacant. Barely an hour before Dwayne's arrival, Zeb had learned that another of the chain's buyers was to move into the opening that Zeb had expected for himself. So great was his disappointment, and his resulting distraction, that he had scarcely heard a word that Dwayne had spoken. In fact, Zeb had made an initial contact for a position elsewhere; and under those circumstances he had virtually no interest in Dwayne's project.

Zeb's reaction to his bad news was a decisive factor in the selling situation that Dwayne had entered into with such great confidence. Despite the clues he should have recognized in Zeb's behavior, Dwayne had done nothing to alter his selling to meet the requirements of the situation, and the result was a serious failure.

Mastering Personal Factors in the Selling Situation

As the preceding example suggests, the prospect may be affected by a variety of factors, including matters of personal concern. It is only common sense to realize that people with serious problems are not as likely to be as receptive as they might otherwise be.

The salesperson meeting a prospect for the first time has no sure way of knowing if the prospect is acting in an unusual way; and the salesperson who has met the prospect before cannot tell if a change in behavior is due to factors which are temporary, or likely to have a continuing effect. In addition, it is only natural for a salesperson to assume that the prospect's behavior is due to something the salesperson has done or said.

It can help greatly, before a first call, to learn as much as possible about the prospect you intend to see, so that you know something of what to expect. After a meeting in which you find the prospect's general attitude difficult, it is a good idea to make inquiries to find out what you can do about it before the next meeting.

A salesperson should develop the ability to assess whether he or she is "getting through" to the prospect—whether the prospect is really listening; and understanding what the salesperson is saying; whether the particular approach, vocabulary, tone, emphasis, etc. are truly appropriate to *this* prospect, under *these* conditions. A salesperson should be sensitive to the specific effectiveness of his or her selling effort, and to what alterations in his or her selling can make it more effective with a particular prospect, in a particular selling situation. (This is more fully discussed later in this chapter, pages 64-67.)

A salesperson should always be aware of the time dimension, especially as affected by the prospect's commitments and attitude. Prospects are often under time constraints: upcoming appointments; or a sense of urgency about work deadlines or unfinished tasks; or even the general pressure of things to be done. For the salesperson to take up too much time under such conditions may do more harm than even the most effective selling can overcome.

A salesperson should also have a sense of timing; not only in the presentation of *Communication* about *Benefits*, for instance (Chapter 6), but also for the suitability of the particular occasion.

Example: The Right Time and the Wrong Time

Ida Jackson sells office furniture. She has an appointment at 2:30 for her first meeting with Cliff Gregson, office manager of the home office of the Nelson Insurance Agency. At 2:25 she gives her card to Grace Pullman, the receptionist, and waits to be called in.

At 2:45 she asks Grace if there may be much more of a delay.

"I really don't know," Grace answers, "but if Mr. Gregson doesn't call you in soon, I'll go find out."

Ida thanks her and waits. After about ten minutes Grace walks to the office door and opens it. Ida hears her say, "Mr. Gregson, Ms. Jackson is here for her 2:30 appointment." There is an answering mumble. Grace closes the door, returns to her seat and says to Ida: "Go on in."

Something in the way she says it makes Ida reply: "He doesn't sound like he's in a very good mood. . . ."

Grace looks at her, smiles, hesitates, and then replies: "There were some problems this morning."

Ida returns the smile and steps into the office.

Although Gregson is courteous and invites Ida to go ahead with her presentation, Ida detects signs of inattention and distraction. The man is only half-listening. Clearly, his mind is on something else. Ida decides to act on that perception and interrupts herself.

"Mr. Gregson," Ida says, "I have a feeling that this isn't a very good time for me to be talking to you about what we can do for this office. It isn't something I can cover in five minutes. It's about saving space with our Super-Cubicles, increasing office productivity with our Marvel Modules, and improving convenience with our Logistic Layout. You and I would need to walk around together, while I take notes; then I could come up with a detailed proposal that would probably save your company thousands of dollars a year, as well as saving everybody's time and energy.

"That's what I would like to do, but I don't think today is the right day for it. Why don't we make another appointment for a time when you'll be feeling free to spend an hour or so to get me started on the survey—which, of course, will cost you nothing."

Gregson eyes Ida for a moment, and then agrees.

"You happen to be right," Gregson says. "Something came up this morning that I didn't expect when I made this appointment; and it's something I should be taking care of. But I am interested in having you make your survey. We plan to modernize this office in connection with the installation of computerized word processing and the reorganization of our secretarial procedures. We'll probably do over some of our older branches also. And I know what your outfit can do, having seen the new offices of Reliable Insurance, downtown. Why don't you come back—let's see—same time, next Thursday?"

Usually, of course, it is the prerogative of the prospect to bring the interview to a conclusion. But in some selling situations, the prospect feels a sense of obligation to sit and listen to a salesperson, even when the prospect has good reason to do otherwise. There are a number of reasons for this, including the prospect's natural courtesy, a special relationship between the salesperson's company and the prospect's company, and, as in the preceding example, the prospect's recognition of the potential relevance of the salesperson's offering.

But a selling situation may also be allowed to continue only because of the prospect's lack of initiative to terminate it. In such situations the selling effect is likely to be negative because of the prospect's probable resentment at having to sit through a presentation at an inopportune time.

There are other kinds of personal factors in the selling situation, and the salesperson should be alert to them and to their positive potential. For instance, the environment may provide clues to the prospect's personal interests and hobbies. Photographs and other graphics, trophies, books and magazines often indicate how the prospect likes to spend his or her time away from the job. Reference to such activities or interests can be effective in building a *Relationship* and help in adding a certain personal emphasis, when relevant to the selling of *Benefits*. This kind of exploitation of personal factors is more fully discussed in Chapter 6.

This discussion would be incomplete if it did not point out the differences between those meetings of salesperson and prospect which take place by differing introductory arrangements. Here are the possibilities, arranged in decreasing order of contribution to the selling situation:

- Appointment made with the prospect directly by telephone or letter.
- Appointment with the prospect made by the prospect's superior.
- Appointment with the prospect made by the prospect's colleague.
- Appointment with the prospect made by the prospect's secretary or receptionist.
- Call made without appointment during designated calling hours for salespersons.
- "Cold call"—a call made without an appointment and without checking to find out if there are any calling hours.

Problems of Organizational Relationships and How to Handle Them

Some salespersons are faced with selling situations which are complicated by factors in the relationship between the company they represent and the company on which they are calling. The relationship may be ongoing, or it may be a past relationship.

1. *An ongoing relationship.* This may be formal and contractual, or based on an informal "understanding," or based on a record of repeat sales. The prospect's company may make a regular practice of purchasing from the salesperson's company on a nonexclusive basis; or it may be bound to it by contract as a sole supplier, or as a primary or secondary source. Some companies tend to buy from those that buy from them (though "reciprocity" and even "trade relations" may skirt legality as "combinations in restraint of trade"). Corporations will usually prefer to buy from their own subsidiaries, but sometimes they will consider competitive offerings from outside sources and buy from them if the terms are more favorable.

In any such selling situations, the salesperson representing the favored vendor has an assured advantage (even amounting to certainty, under some conditions). But the representative of the purchasing company may not be entirely happy about being compelled to buy from the favored source. He or she may feel the favored supplier is taking unfair advantage of the situation and not fully meeting expectations or obligations. He or she may believe that a potential, but excluded, competitor would be a preferable supplier. He or she may resent being deprived of discretionary authority and being required to deal with the salesperson's company—or the salesperson.

Under such circumstances, the favored salesperson should feel an obligation to "keep it sold"—to act in such a way as to reinforce the favorable arrangements, and to make it advantageous to the customer to continue the relationship. If this is not done, dissatisfaction will grow. Contracts may not be renewed and noncontractual arrangements may be abrogated. Thus the salesperson's job is to make sure that a favorable arrangement remains favorable to the customer. This may require the salesperson to take up with his or her own management the requirements for delivering the benefits expected and keeping the customer satisfied.

2. *A past relationship that has been ended or interrupted.* This may have been due to customer dissatisfaction or to a disagreement of some kind. It may also have been due to a change in the customer's needs or to an advantage gained by a competitive supplier. It may even have resulted from a change in policy, design, or offerings in the salesperson's company.

In such situations, the salesperson seeking to restore the former relationship should be fully informed on the history of the situation and be prepared to discuss it in an objective, nonargumentive manner. If there were elements in the past which caused customer dissatisfaction, the salesperson should undertake to convince the former customer that conditions which gave rise to that dissatisfaction no longer exist and conditions for a new relationship are now entirely favorable.

3. *Special relationships.* Sometimes, the prospect's company has an arrangement with a competitor of the salesperson's company which excludes the salesperson's company from competing for the prospect's business. Such arrangements are vulnerable if the values the salesperson can offer are truly superior, and if this is made convincingly clear to the prospect.

If the opportunity to sell directly is denied, there are ways to sell indirectly. For instance, if the product or service offered by the salesperson's company is purchased by major competitors of the prospect company, someone in that company will learn of it—especially if it is reported or publicized in a business publication. Such indirect selling is standard practice and is usually effective.

Of course, it is also possible to "make an end run" around specially favored competition by offering something which the competitor cannot. This is usually beyond the power of the salesperson alone, who could, nevertheless, propose it to his or her management.

Example: Innovating Around the Competition

Blair Gossage represents Lakeland Electrodes, a small but energetic company which is trying to enter the market for graphite electrodes. The volume possibilities lie with the major steel mills, and they all have long-term relations with the two major suppliers. Lakeland is trying hard to break in but has received only a few token orders.

Now Lakeland has retained a consultant who has developed a new and helpful service—a well thought-out program for training furnace personnel in ways that can ensure superior electrode performance. Blair has offered this program to "Melter" Peck, who is in charge of furnace operations at a major steel mill. Peck has seen a demonstration of the Lakeland program and is now trying to persuade Eustace Molson, vice president-purchasing, to open the door to Lakeland.

"Eustace, Imperial and Royal have had all our electrode business, and they expect to continue getting it. So, they haven't any incentive to do any more than they have to do. But Lakeland needs the business, and they're going after it the right way. The new service they offer is good, and it could improve our productivity. Imperial and Royal have nothing like it. I don't believe they even think that way. Eustace, I *want* that Lakeland program for our mills. What do you say?"

Eustace Molson reluctantly agreed, and "Melter" Peck called Blair in and gave him the go-ahead. The Lakeland program was a success; Blair began to get substantial orders for Lakeland electrodes.

Making the Most of the Physical Environment

When you are in the prospect's office, you have the opportunity to observe evidence of his or her personal interests and activities. Photographs of the prospect's family and of the prospect engaged in sport or hobby activities are obvious take-off points for questions or comments that not only help you to learn about the "Whole Person" you are dealing with, but also to enhance the *Relationship*. Trophies, diplomas, framed certificates and documents, and other items can inform and serve as "conversation pieces." But there can be a great deal more to such exploitation of the physical environment than that, and a competent salesperson can usually find a way to utilize such personal items to build understanding and *Relationship*, and to introduce effective *Communication* to bolster the value of the *Benefits* to be offered.

Example: Hitch the Pitch to a Picture

Toby Klein sells components to machine manufacturers. He is making his first call on Ludlow Sikes, vice president-manufacturing of Superdyne Machines. He enters Sikes' office, shakes hands and as he sits, he notices on the wall a framed photo of a Luxo cabin cruiser, with a group of people on board.

"Yours?" he asks Sikes, gesturing at the picture. "What power?" he asks when Sikes acknowledges that the handsome craft is his.

"Twin Soroka diesels—two-fifties," Sikes replies.

"That's a fine engine. We supply Soroka with the main bearings for their crankshafts and connecting rods. Luxo also buys our reduction gearing for the drives to their propeller shafts, and a lot more." Then Toby added with a smile: "So you see, you are already using our products."

"That's interesting, Mr. Klein," says Ludlow. "I'll have to ask Luxo about their experience with your products. Must be satisfactory, since they're still using them."

"They certainly are, Mr. Sikes, and that's not all. You go fishing from that cruiser, and you probably use some Marlow reels, especially for big game fish. Well, we produce parts for the Marlow reels. I also see some children, there, on the bow. I assume they have bicycles? Maybe motor scooters? You'd find our parts in Pedalia bicycles and three lines of scooter, including the Rocket."

Toby is already selling his line without even getting down to business—and all on the basis of his prospect's hobby. He associated what he has to sell with something that has a strong personal connection with the prospect, and that is bound to have a helpful psychological effect.

Here is another example of how a personal item can be used for an effective opening.

Example: Hitch the Pitch to a Diploma

Elaine Soble sells electronic office equipment for the Automoffice Corporation. She is calling on Norma Rimble, who is vice president of Multi-Bank Holdings, in charge of data processing. Elaine sees the framed diplomas on the office wall in back of Norma and notes one particularly.

"I see you have a degree from the University of Michigan," Elaine says. "The president of our company, Mort Bangs, went to Michigan. Maybe you remember him—he was an All-American line backer; they called him 'Mortal' Bangs."

"Of course I remember him. I used to see him play when I was a freshman. I even danced with him once or twice, at parties. The girls all thought he was great!"

"They still do—though he's married and has four kids," Elaine says.

"So—that beautiful jock is president of Automoffice now," Norma says with a smile. "You might say 'hello' to him for me; he might remember me. Now, tell me about Mort's company."

If Elaine had not picked up on that diploma, she would have had to make a formal start on her selling. Now, in the "reflected glow" of Norma's memories, Elaine's *Communication* will meet a friendlier reception.

Elaine was taking a long shot when she told Norma that the president of her company was a well-known alumnus of Michigan; but she had nothing to lose. Suppose Norma had answered that she did not remember "Mortal" Bangs—would that have hurt? Elaine would have simply picked up from there with no harm done.

The only risk was if Norma had an adverse feeling about Bangs. That could have hurt Elaine's chances of making a sale. But that was an unlikely possibility.

When salespeople accompany prospects into other company environments, beyond the prospect's office (other offices, plants, laboratories, branches, warehouses, company planes, etc.), much can be learned from observation of the relations between the prospect and other individuals in the company. Such relations can provide valuable clues to the prospect's status and influence with other elements of the organization, the involvement of others in the buying decision, and the values and interests they may bring to bear on that decision.

Meetings in other environments include the many kinds of "neutral" places where salespersons and prospects may meet or go together, such as restaurants, bars, theaters, sports arenas, conferences, conventions, etc. Also to be considered are those environments related to the salesperson, such as the display rooms, offices, exhibits, hospitality suites, etc., of the organization that the salesperson represents.

When meeting in a prospect's home, the salesperson may have major opportunities to develop insights into the interests and character of the prospect, and the insights gained can be extremely useful in making a sale. Many such opportunities will be similar to those suggested for the prospect's office. But there is an interesting difference: people tend to display in their offices items that fit in with their images of themselves and that, in their view, project those images to others; in most homes the visiting salesperson will find many other sources of information—some obvious, and some not so obvious—about the Whole Prospect. And making use of such information is a challenge that a good salesperson welcomes.

First Impressions and
the Problem of Prejudice

First impressions are important, especially in situations which do not provide opportunities for further meetings, in the course of which unfavorable first impressions could be overcome. Every salesperson wants to make a favorable first impression, but conditions may stand in the way. Some of the conditions which create unfavorable first impressions are unavoidable, unforeseeable, and out of the salesperson's control. But other conditions which may create unfavorable first impressions can be foreseen and, occasionally, circumvented.

In "conflict of personalities," two people are viewed as incompatible because each represents to the other a set of characteristics which have been disliked in others. There is also the psychological phenomenon of "stereotype" in which a person "sees" certain characteristics—usually those disliked—in other people, even when they do not have those characteristics. Stereotyping often works against those who are members of racial and religious minorities. Stereotyping may also center on nationality, age (for example, intolerance of some older people for youngsters, and vice versa), sex (perceived sexual characteristics or proclivities), and cultural levels or origins (as indicated by dress, accent, choice, and pronunciation of words). In addition, stereotyping may be directed against people who are tall or short, fat or lean; there are even those who react to people according to the color of hair.

There is little the salesperson can do to overcome such prejudices before a first meeting. But sometimes the prejudiced prospect conducts a functioning business relationship with the salesperson or with the organization the salesperson represents because the prospect needs what the salesperson is offering or because the prospect's organization makes it advisable for the prospect to deal with the salesperson's organization. If others in the prospect's organization are involved in the buying decision, the salesperson can "outflank" the prejudiced prospect by selling them the product or service. Occasionally prejudiced persons make exceptions of those they have come to know and esteem.

The first meeting between salesperson and prospect, and the first impression of the salesperson formed by the prospect, will be affected by other factors. Among these are the prospect's knowledge and reaction to the organization represented by the prospect; the reputation of the salesperson's company; previous contacts with others representing or connected with the company (especially predecessors of the present salesperson); and the nature of the arrangements that preceded the meeting.

The salesperson should arrive informed as fully as possible about any previous relations that may be relevant, and should be prepared to refer to or react to any reference to these in such a way as to make his or her presence seem constructive. For instance:

"Yes, I know Roy called on you for years and understood your problems and gave you excellent service. I'm not Roy, of course, but I'm going to do my best to serve you in the same way."

"Well, I understand there was a problem some years ago with some of the variable speed controls made before we installed the new testing program. But it couldn't happen now—and here's why."

"You haven't heard of us yet because we're new. Our company was set up only a year ago, to take advantage of new technology. But our management is very experienced; and I used to be with the industry leader. I left them because this company offers a much better opportunity; and I want to tell you why we're going to be the new leader of the industry."

But the circumstances under which the first meeting is arranged can vary so greatly, and usually rest so completely on the initiative of the salesperson, that they deserve special consideration.

Example: Selling the Big Ticket

Brent Leggett is regional sales representative for Titan Constructors, a firm that specializes in building the large long-legged platforms that are used for drilling oil and gas wells in the sea. He is calling on the president of Planetary Petroleum in Denver, Colorado, which recently acquired leases on extensive acreage at sea, off the coast of Malaysia, and which is planning a substantial drilling program.

This is Brent's first call on Planetary, and the appointment was made by Titan's chairman; they are old friends and have occasionally worked together on various "deals." Brent is accompanied by the head of Titan's engineering staff and three of his department managers.

As they land in Titan's plane at Planetary's private air-field, they are met by Planetary's vice president-field operations and are driven to a meeting with Planetary's president and six other Planetary officers. They will be guests in the nearby Planetary Guest House during their three-day stay, during which they will obtain the information necessary to develop their bid-proposal. Three other competitors will also have their representatives at the meeting.

Brent Leggett and his associates are well aware that the impression they make and the questions they ask will probably be weighed along with the formal bid-proposal when Planetary makes its buying decision.

Example: Selling the Small Ticket

Skip Carlson sells vacuum cleaners, door to door. His assigned territory is in a section of the city that has mostly multi-story apartment houses. Skip usually has to get permission to get past the doorman in those buildings that seem to have the best prospects, and he usually does this by getting an appointment with one of the tenants. Once admitted, and after keeping the appointment, Skip takes the elevator to the top floor; then he works his way down through the building, systematically. Skip works strictly on commission. One sale a day will keep him going, and he averages a sale for every 30 calls. Of course, the more calls he makes, the more he will sell.

Many kinds of people live in the apartment houses and, therefore, the situations differ from door to door. Some women peer at him through a peephole, ask who is there, and tell him they are not interested. Others open the door a few inches on a chain bolt, and some of them let him in.

Skip understands that the prospect's first glimpse of him and his first words are important. So he dresses respectably and starts each encounter with a tried beginning, featuring the phrase "free demonstration." He usually sells about half of those prospects who allow him to demonstrate the vacuum cleaner.

Sometimes Skip tries 60 or more doors a day; gets in to talk to 10 or 12 women, conducts 2 to 4 demonstrations, and sells one or two vacuum cleaners.

There's a world of difference between the selling situations that face Brent Leggett and Skip Carlson, but they both understand the importance of the first impression they make on a prospect, and they both try to make it favor a sale.

Feedback: Key to Understanding
the Selling Situation

When two people are talking to one another, everything that each of them says reflects some of what is in his or her mind. What is in the mind of the speaker at the moment is not only the current situation, but some of the past experience of the speaker, which comes to the speaker's mind in reaction to the current situation.

Whatever a prospect says in response to what you say, or on his own initiative, owes its content and form to such factors as these:

1. The prospect's reaction to what you have just said.
2. The prospect's reaction to what you said before.
3. The prospect's tendency to support, defend, or follow-up on what he or she said before.
4. The prospect's self-image.
5. The way the prospect feels about himself or herself.
6. The prospect's feelings and thoughts about you.
7. The prospect's feelings and thoughts about the current situation.
8. The prospect's interest in what you are trying to sell.
9. The prospect's feelings and thoughts about the company you represent and the competition.
10. The prospect's attitude toward situations he may regard as similar to the current one.
11. The prospect's needs and wants, or understanding of the needs and wants of others in the organization.
12. The prospect's feelings and thoughts about his or her job, organization, and position and status in it.

Of course, any or all of these factors may affect the behavior of the prospect at the same time, but not with equal force. Sometimes one factor is paramount, as when a thought or feeling comes through strongly enough to find expression largely undiluted by the effects of other factors. When a person is angry, excited, enthusiastic, or extremely interested, they tend to concentrate on the subject under discussion; when that happens, of course, it is easy to get a good idea of where they stand on the subject. On the other hand, when a person is not driven by such strong feelings, what they say can be influenced by the slightest reaction to almost any idea. Then it becomes difficult to learn much about their underlying thoughts or feelings.

When you are planning a sales call, you should look over the list of factors above (and try to think of others that may influence the situation), and then try to forecast which factors are most likely to be at work in determining what the prospect says and does, and what factors would be most favorable to you.

For instance, suppose you are going to see a purchasing agent for the first time. You need to work toward getting his thoughts on #8 and #11, but you know that other factors may have some effect on the situation, even before you start selling. Which factors will get in the way? How should you deal with them? And, assuming that you do get to #8 and #11, what is the best way to reach an agreement?

There is only one way you can find out the answers to such questions— you have to get them from what the prospect says and does. Seldom will you find out by asking the prospect directly! Generally, you will have to rely on what the prospect says and how he acts.

So, when you communicate with the prospect, you should do so not only to give the information that you are there to give, but also to get the prospect to respond in such a way as to "tell" you what you need to know in order to make the presentation that will be *most effective* for *this* prospect in *this* situation. What you say can *elicit* the information you need from the prospect—if you understand the principle of *feedback* and if you know how to make good use of it.

Many people appreciate the importance of feedback, but do not fully realize that you can do more than just take what you get of it—you can get what you need of it, if you know how.

And many people appreciate the importance of listening, and preach the importance of it. But you need to do more than listen; you need to understand, evaluate, interpret, relate and correlate.

Example: Time Is Not for Wasting

> SALESPERSON: Mr. Gadsby, our line of neutralizing gear enhancers is the best on the market.
> PURCHASING AGENT: What's a neutralizing whatchamacallit?
> SALESPERSON: Oh? I thought you use them on your rotating motivators.
> PURCHASING AGENT: Do we?

(Salesperson goes into a long "spiel" to inform the P.A. about his company's line of rotating motivators and the volume of their purchases of gear enhancers from competitor companies. But the P.A. isn't interested because this purchasing is not done by him. He didn't know about it because it is handled through a long-term contract negotiated by his boss. The salesperson is wasting his time, and the sooner he finds this out, the better for all concerned.)

Example: More Than Listening

> SALESWOMAN: Mr. Greenwood, everybody in the trade knows you're buying your semi-metallic gribbles from Flormac.
>
> PURCHASING AGENT: And you'd like some of the action?
>
> SALESWOMAN: I can show you where you'd be better off with us.
>
> PURCHASING AGENT: Price-wise?
>
> SALESWOMAN: Price-wise and quality-wise.
>
> PURCHASING AGENT: How do you know what we pay Flormac for their gribbles?
>
> SALESWOMAN: I know we can sell them for $68 a pair and $53 a pair in quantity.
>
> PURCHASING AGENT: Hm. . . . $53 a pair, you say?
>
> SALESWOMAN: In the quantities you're interested in, Mr. Greenwood. Like I said, $53 a pair! And our gribbles have purer silica.
>
> PURCHASING AGENT: Let's see, now. . . . How about 900 pairs, delivered in October?

This clever saleswoman exploited feedback which told her that the purchasing agent was interested in gribbles of competitive or better quality at a price of $53. Now she is on her way to working out a large sale.

How Feedback Tells You the Possible Deal

Example: The No-Selling, No Feedback Deal

You are driving from one town to another. You are hungry and in a hurry, so you decide to grab a quick hamburger. Up ahead is a familiar fast-food place, and you pull in. You already know what you want and how much it costs. You don't have to look at the menu, posted on the walls, because you are familiar with it. So you give your order to the attendant at the counter and lay down the exact change.

This place does its selling mainly by being there and looking like a thousand other franchisees of the same large corporation (which does a lot of TV advertising). There is no salesperson-to-prospect selling: every prospect makes his own deal from the available selection of items at the posted prices. The people at the counter only deliver what is ordered and take the money.

There is little need for *Communication* because the prospect already has a good idea of the *Benefits* and has decided to buy. The only *Relationship* that counts here is between the prospect and the image which the corporation gives to its franchisees. Although you have never been in this particular place before, you know what to expect. You know exactly what deals you can make, and you, the prospect, decide which one you want. They don't need a salesperson to sell it to you. You could say that every vehicle on this road carries at least one prospect; and the vehicles that stop let out predetermined customers.

Now, for a little contrast.

Example: The Months-of-Feedback Deal

The Gruber Exploration Corporation needs an executive jet plane for its senior executives to get around to its widely scattered drilling sites and business conferences. Jeffrey Todd represents Mongol Aviation, and he wants to sell the Gruber people a Super-Mongol. A month ago he made a full-dress presentation to a group of Gruber executives. Now he is here to get their feedback. Jeff is in conference with Fred Harris, executive vice-president of Gruber, and five other Gruber executives.

"We called you back in, Jeff," Harris tells him, "because we now think we might go with Mongol, if we can be satisfied on a few important points."

"You know we'll do all we can, Mr. Harris," Jeff says. "I'm glad you realize how right our Super-Mongol K would be for you."

"No, Jeff, not the K. We don't need that capacity. Six seats are all we need, not twelve."

"You're thinking of our Model R?"

"No, that hasn't got the range we need. We're thinking of your Model B, with extra fuel tanks, and with the cabin modified to take only six of those rotating seats."

"We can do that OK. We turned out something like that for Jasper Global."

"We know; we've looked at that plane. But that's not all. We want a larger baggage compartment."

"I think there'd be room for that without even modifying the fuselage," says Jeff.

"Fine. We've also decided to trade in our Space-Master. Joe, here, can give you the specifications and arrange to have it flown to your plant for your inspection."

"The sooner the better," Jeff says. "But the market is pretty weak now for old prop-jets."

"I hope not. We are very much concerned about the overall price, the trade-in allowance, the date of delivery, and the overall terms—like how much down, how much on delivery, and so forth. I should also tell you that you're competing with Loyalty Flightmasters. We're telling them just what we're telling you, because we think their Flightmistress C could be modified to meet our needs. So we'd like to have a formal, detailed proposal from you, giving us an option between the Planetary L-141 and the Zodiac Z-42 engines. We'd consider a three- or even a five-year maintenance contract, too."

"OK," Jeff says. "I'll get back to you by—say—May 14th."

"Our board meets on the 12th."

"I'll have the proposal to you before then."

"I suggest you plan to meet with us here on the 10th, and your proposal ought to be here by the 8th."

"We'll do it."

This dialogue is fairly typical of Jeff's selling situations. The executive jets he sells cost a lot of money, and they frequently have to be modified to meet customer requirements. Selling executive jets has virtually nothing in common with selling hamburgers; Jeff has to find out from the prospect what kind of deal the prospect will consider before he can start to put together a deal that can be sold. And finding out what only the prospect can tell requires feedback.

The skill of selling involves knowing what feedback you need from the prospect, how to get the feedback you need, how to understand and evaluate the feedback you get, and what to do about it.

Example: How to Lose Part of the Possible Deal

Oscar Peebles is a salesman for Nisbet Adornments, manufacturers of costume jewelry and similar lines. He sells mainly to drug stores, supermarkets, and other retailers which do not specialize in jewelry. But he also acts as a commission agent for both Scintilla Gems, a manufacturer of higher priced lines, and for Tempo, Inc., importers of moderately priced watches, both of which lines he usually sells to jewelry stores.

Oscar is calling on the specialties buyer for a chain of supermarkets who has been a regular customer for gold-plated chains, charms, rings, and other low-bracket trinkets, and who is now giving him a detailed order for the faster-moving items of the Nisbet line.

"Thanks for the order," says Oscar. "Can I interest you in anything else?"

"We're thinking of expanding our specialty department lines," answers the buyer. "Any suggestions?"

Oscar, his thoughts concentrated on the Nisbet line and on the detailed orders he has just received, responds by suggesting some additional Nisbet items that the buyer has never ordered. Oscar shows samples and pictures, and the buyer agrees to small, trial orders of some of these. So Oscar feels good about his sale.

A month later Oscar is about to call on the same buyer again and on the way, he stops off at one of the chain's stores to look over the specialty department. He is looking to see how the Nisbet line is displayed—especially the new items. But, to his surprise, he sees that much of the shelf space is taken up by displays of higher priced jewelry from competitors of Scintilla Gems and of watches from a competitor of Tempo.

Oscar feels resentment that the buyer didn't give him a chance to compete for these lines, and when he makes his call, he gives vent to this feeling:

"Why didn't you tell me you were putting in those higher priced lines?'

"Come on, Oscar! I *told* you we were thinking of expanding our specialty departments. I even gave you some orders for items we never bought before."

"You didn't tell me you were going into higher price brackets. I'm an agent for Scintilla and Tempo, and both of them have lines as good as, or better than, the ones you bought—and fully competitive, price-wise."

"Oscar, I gave you all the information you needed—all I gave anybody. I told you we would be expanding our specialty departments; and I was ready and willing to look at and consider anything you could offer. But you didn't offer me anything from Scintilla or Tempo."

Oscar missed out on some profitable sales because he didn't get what he should have from the buyer's feedback. Oscar heard it, but he didn't understand it fully or evaluate it adequately. Worst of all, he didn't try to get more feedback. (For example, by simply asking: "What sort of lines are you thinking of going into?" or "How about trying a display of Scintilla or Tempo?")

Yes, Oscar did make some extra sales in the Nisbet line on the basis of feedback from the buyer. But he missed the chance to sell the Scintilla and Tempo lines because he didn't take full advantage of the feedback. Many salespersons do that—make a sale on the basis of only a partial grasp of the meaning of the feedback they receive. Like Oscar, they "kick themselves" later when they realize what they missed and why.

Knowing what kind of deal you can make with a prospect is often essential to making any deal at all, and the way to find out what deal you can make—and should aim at making—is through feedback from the prospect. It is essential to listen, but you should also understand feedback, evaluate it, get more of it (if you need it), and think carefully about what it really means.

How to Use Feedback
to Do Your Best Selling

Every prospect is different, and there are as many best ways to sell as there are prospects. But every salesperson is also different; so the best way for one salesperson to sell to a particular prospect would differ from the best way another salesperson would sell to the same prospect. In addition, the best way to sell to a prospect varies with the nature of the product or service. It should also vary to match the particular state of the prospect's mood, changing personal situation, current conflicting, parallel, or supportive circumstances, etc.

You can see that there is a whole universe of variables within which the selling process can take any form or pattern, with many possible degrees of appropriateness or inappropriateness. How, then, does the professional salesperson go about selling with maximum effect?

Example: Adapting the Selling Approach

Brent Standish sells boilers, primarily those used to heat buildings. He is making his first call on Ian MacTavish, the irascible head of MacTavish Engineers, a substantial firm specializing in the installation of steam and hot water heating systems. Brent walks into this greeting:

"So you're the young feller that idiot Andrew McGinnis has sent to tell me about boilers!"

Brent immediately understands that he is up against a crusty old-timer who will resent and resist most selling attempts. But the old man has built-up a large, successful firm. He must be shrewd, and he must know plenty. A prospect like that, given the chance, will often sell himself. So Brent rapidly adapts his selling approach.

"Mr. MacTavish," Brent begins, as he places a brochure on his desk, "I know you were buying and installing boilers long before I even learned what they are; so *I* won't try to tell *you* why our new boilers are the most efficient and the easiest to install. I only ask you to look at this diagram, to see the new shape, the new arrangement of the tubes, and the new form of the firebox. And maybe you'll have a question about our new electronic controls."

MacTavish grunts, picks up the brochure, scowls, and studies the diagram for a moment.

"How much is this Mark VII?" he growls. Brent tells him, and there is a long pause. Then:

"Somebody in your shop must know something," says MacTavish. "That's the first time I've seen a boiler made the way they should be made. Just tell me where I can see some of them in use, and I'll see if they work as well as they should. Meanwhile, go back to that old fool McGinnis, and tells him MacTavish wants his best low price for ten, twenty, or fifty of these. If he has any sense left, we may do some business. I'm holding onto this paper."

Brent left while he was ahead, glad that he had not started a "regular" sales pitch and thus avoided: "Young man, I was installing boilers when you were still in didies. Don't try to tell me . . . ."

There is an old saying about never underrating the intelligence of people; prospects are usually more intelligent than they may appear to a salesperson. If they feel that you are "talking down" to them, they will not like it and they may seriously resent it. One of the most important values of feedback is to determine the best level for addressing the prospect. It should not be so simple as to insult his or her intelligence, and not so advanced as to be "over his (or her) head."

Remember, also, the important difference between *intelligence* and *knowledge*. Some intelligent prospects may know little about what you are trying to sell, but they can easily and quickly "take in" what you tell them. On the other hand, some prospects may have had a lot of experience with what you are selling, but aren't very bright when it comes to understanding some of the points you are trying to make.

Professional salespeople are sensitive to such differences and know how to adjust and adapt the selling process to the levels of knowledge and intelligence of the prospect. If you do a good job of it and make your selling interesting, so the prospects are conscious of the relevance of what you are saying to their own values, they will bring their own knowledge to bear on what you say. But if you are telling them what they already know, or if you talk to them in a way so elementary that their minds begin to drift, you will surely lose them.

And if you talk "over their heads," you will not do much selling. Only feedback can tell you how the prospect is reacting to you. The more sensitive you are to the feedback and the sooner you adapt and adjust—until the feedback tells you that you are on target—the more successful your selling will be.

It would be easy to sell if you could "read the mind" of the prospect. You would know what to say and the best way to say it. Feedback gives you a way to read the prospect's mind. Most prospects will provide all the feedback you need, if you give them a chance. Get the feedback you need, listen to it, understand it, evaluate it—and use it!

This is the basic way to a better *Relationship* with the prospect; the right *Communication* to do the selling; the right emphasis on *Benefits*—and therefore the maximum Motivational Selling Leverage—with each individual prospect.

Mastering the Selling Situation with Feedback

To put this matter of mastering the selling situation in a general perspective, let us list only a few of the large number of possible situations in which you may be making your selling effort.

1. You do not know it, but the person you are addressing has no interest in what you want to sell.

2. You do not know it, but the person you are addressing has only a slight "possible" or "future" interest in what you want to sell.

3. You do not know it, but the person you are addressing is, in fact, not the right person to see about buying what you want to sell.

4. The person you are addressing is a prospect for what you want to sell, but you do not know that he or she already has another, regular and satisfactory source of supply—one of your competitors.

5. You do not know that the person you are addressing is not a prospect for what you are trying to sell but may be a prospect for something else in your line.

There we have five very different situations—and these and many others can often occur, with an infinitely great number of possible variations. But let us just take these five. Given the situations as outlined, what is the best result that you could achieve with each one?

1. You should find out as soon as possible that this person is not really a prospect.

2. You should identify that "possible" or "future" interest, learn as much as you can about it, decide what you can do about it, and establish a *Relationship* to support an effective follow-up.

3. Establish a *Relationship* with this "wrong" person that will enable you to get as much information as possible about the prospective sale and about the right person to see.

4. You need to find out everything you can that will enable you to compete more effectively, or that will at least give you a crack at becoming a secondary source of supply.

5. You will want to find out what it is that you can sell to this prospect.

Obviously, you will need appropriate feedback in all of these situations. But each requires a different kind of information, which you will need if you are to do a good job of selling. To get the feedback you need that will provide you with this information, you have to fulfill certain conditions. The person you are talking to will have to feel like giving you this information, which means you have to establish a *Relationship* that provides the right motivation for him or her to do so. But that may not be enough. You may have to give some information yourself to get the prospect thinking along the most appropriate lines. You may have to cue additional statements, ask the right questions, encourage further talk, show interest and express appreciation. All this must be done with two objectives in mind: to follow the line of inquiry that brings you the information that can help you make a sale; and to reinforce the *Relationship*. Following these two objectives may pull you in different directions.

Therefore, unless you are quite sure you already know enough about a particular situation to do a good job of selling, the best policy is to aim at building a favorable *Relationship*, and then being *very* open, attentive, flexible, and responsive. In brief, unless you believe that no exploration is needed, make your opening "invitingly exploratory."

There is another perspective in which to view a selling situation. The prospect is giving time, attention, and information. What are *you* giving? A good *Relationship* is based on give and take, a fair exchange. A good *Relationship* must benefit *both* sides. Being polite, courteous—even charming or amusing—may be helpful to you and may be enough for the short term. But, if the *Relationship* is to continue on a level that will really be helpful to you, there has to be more. The *Relationship* must also be helpful to the other person.

Often the easiest and best way to be helpful is to provide information. Of course, this can be "packaged" information, printed by your organization. There is also information that is provided to meet a request or to anticipate a need that *you* have foreseen, and there is information that you have accidentally picked up or have had the "initiative" to dig up on your own. Of the two kinds of information, "packaged" and "personal," it is not difficult to figure out which is more appreciated and the more likely to contribute substantially to your image as a helpful person, and thus build or reinforce a good *Relationship*.

In the mind of the prospect, the image of helpfulness is one that can do a salesperson a lot of good. It is well worth a lot of thought and effort to find ways of building such an image.

★★ 5 ★★

Selling Leverage:
New Key to
Overcoming Objections

Positive Motivation and Its
Importance in the Decision to Buy

AXIOM A: There is no such thing as a "true sale" without *positive* motivation. Some people can be bull-dozed, hypnotized, seduced, misled, deceived, or pushed into a purchase they would not otherwise make. Basically, however, people will not buy what they do not need or like.

Some people are extremely vulnerable to "impulse buying," and some salespersons have an extraordinary ability to stimulate quick-buying decisions. They make a great success of door-to-door selling or of hawking specialty merchandise on street corners or on TV ("Call 1-800- . . . NOW!"). They know how to convert "non-prospects" into customers, who may decide, after an "impulse" purchase, that they do not need or like what they bought; and some may return it, demanding their money back, but they did feel differently when that "impulse" made them buy.

When a person wants something, and wants it without any doubt or question, we may assume that such a person is either in love, is full of ambition for some promotion or achievement, or is a "red-hot" prospect to buy.

Example: The Positively Motivated Celebrity

Jefferson Trendle is a junior salesman in the Rolls-Royce salesroom on Michigan Boulevard. He is only supposed to help out the "old-timers," the veteran salespeople. But when a "certain well-known person" came into the showroom, shortly after noon, all the old-timers were out to lunch.

The celebrity advances purposefully toward the elegant "Silver Ghost," a Rolls-Royce, which occupies the place of honor on the showroom floor and exclaims: "That's what I want! and I want it now!" The celebrity then produces $90,000 in cash, plus an extra $1000 to hire Jeff as his chauffeur for the rest of the day.

When the old-timers return from lunch, they find a vacancy on the showroom floor, a jubilant note from Jefferson, and a deposit slip for $90,000 from the bank next door.

Of course, Jeff didn't *sell* that Rolls. He didn't have to, because that celebrity was already loaded with positive motivation.

Fortunately, salespeople sometimes find that kind of positive motivation in customers who approach them. The motivation in such situations may be long, pent-up demand or impulse. The occasion may be catching sight of an object that stimulates the desire to own, the enthusiastic recommendation of a friend or neighbor, or the desire to own something like that owned by the boss or some other admired or envied figure. Even an advertisement can do it, sometimes.

In any case, such prospects need no "selling"—only "arranging." They can be exacting and unreasonable about packaging, delivery, extras, colors, sizes, modifications, and terms of payment. But, basically, they are "pre-sold" because of their positive motivation to buy.

Sometimes a new product generates that kind of demand; so can a major price cut. Certain other developments, not easy to anticipate, can send eager purchasers after items that have not been especially in demand before. A new fashion, a popular movie, or a newspaper article may set off a wave of positive motivation to buy.

That kind of "mind made up!" "know what I want!" "gotta have it!" attitude is typical of positive motivation, and selling to people in that frame of mind doesn't require salespersonship. What does require salespersonship is to get people who are not pre-sold into a similar condition of positive motivation.

Of course, the majority of prospects do not have such positive motivation as the celebrity who bought the Rolls-Royce. In general, the prospect fits into one of these categories:

Retail:
(a) He or she has a fairly definite notion of the sort of thing he or she wants, and hopes to find it at a reasonable price. This may be termed "the purposeful shopping syndrome."

(b) He or she has a general interest in buying "something," and is "just looking around" until, maybe, something he or she happens to see causes a more specific notion to crystallize.

(c) He or she was not conscious of a desire or intention to buy anything until he or she saw something, or a salesperson offered something, that appealed to him or her.

Wholesale:

(d) A purchasing agent for a manufacturing concern is under the necessity of identifying and purchasing parts, components, equipment, or services that (1) meet specific requirements set by others; (2) are likely to satisfy operational requirements; (3) can be purchased at acceptable prices and under usual terms; and (4) come from reliable, reputable suppliers.

(e) A professional buyer must find and negotiate for products that conform to the image and merchandising pattern of the store or chain at a cost that will allow a satisfactory mark-up and a price that will attract customers.

(f) The professional buyer becomes aware of the availability of something not previously sought or budgeted for, but which may be advantageous for the organization to acquire.

The salesperson must deal with such prospects as those represented by a, b, d, and e, and bring them from the stage of tentative or generalized interest to that of positive motivation.

The oldest, wisest but also the most misunderstood cliché in the literature of selling is: "Sell the benefits!" But to do this effectively you must first understand what the benefits are to *each* prospect. If you know that, go ahead! But it isn't always clear. Lots of salespersons waste their time doing a wonderful job of selling the wrong benefits—or even of selling the right benefits in the wrong way. This problem is suggested by the expression: "You have to find the right button."

When you emphasize benefits that may be important to you and others, but that are not especially valued by the prospect you are trying to sell, you may be doing little or nothing to increase positive motivation. On the other hand, if you take the trouble to find out what the prospect really values—what he or she truly needs, wants, and likes—then you will have the clue you need to start building the positive motivation that will make the sale.

It is the function of the competent salesperson to uncover such needs, wants, and likes; and to lead the way to a purchase that will satisfy such needs, wants, and likes; and to do this by building positive motivation toward that purchase on the basis of its value for satisfying those needs, wants and likings—which the competent salesperson has been able to bring to the surface.

Motivational Selling Leverage can play a major part in helping the competent salesperson enhance his or her selling power; from the initial contact with the prospect, to the relationship that helps to build up Positive Motivation; to the focusing on Motivational *Selling* Leverage.

Why "Natural Selling" Produces More Positive Motivation Than "Forced Selling"

There is a good men's clothing store in Detroit where two of the salespeople exemplify sharply different ways of selling.

Example: When a Sale Is Not a Sale

Norm Hopkins is "a hell of a salesman." Practically every man that approaches him ends up buying something, whether they intended to or not; and sometimes they buy a lot. Some months, Norm is the top sales-man—writes up more sales than any of the others. The only trouble is, much of it is returned. And—unfortunately—Norm doesn't get much repeat business. He can be extraordinarily persuasive, even charming; and he puts on just enough pressure to get results. But, much of the time, his customers seem to end up with merchandise they don't want to keep. Whatever positive notion they had about buying seems to fade away.

Example: Sales that "Stick"

Lew Haynes handles his customers very differently from Norm. He looks at them carefully and notices various details: how they stand, walk, sit, and lounge; their basic build; their complexions, and a great deal more. He thoughtfully selects several suits to try on them in front of a three-panel mirror. He studies the effects and discusses their feelings about the pattern, color, fabric, weave, style, and fit. He listens attentively, and then tries with another carefully chosen suit.

Lew's customers often ask him to help them pick out ties and shirts to go with the new suit. Sometimes they buy more than one suit, although they hadn't planned to. Lew's customers usually come back and ask for him, and they often bring friends or send them to Lew. There are very few returns; the positive motivation of Lew's customers seems to last.

Figuring only the sales that stay sold, Lew outsells Norm by a con-siderable margin.

Now, it is clear that both Norm and Lew are good at building positive motivation to buy. But it is also clear that Lew's way works out best, in the long run, because the positive motivation he builds lasts.

Let us examine the difference between Norm and Lew's selling.

First, *Relationship*. Norm comes across as a very confident, positive authority. He seems to inspire confidence in many new customers, and he informs them in no uncertain terms about what they should wear and why. When he tells them they look just right, they tend to believe him; and when he states that the suit being tried on is a bargain, they are apt to accept that as a fact.

With many who walk into the store, Norm establishes an immediate *Relationship* based on their recognition of his knowledge, expertise, and his apparent eagerness to see that they buy "the right thing." Some customers, of course, prefer to be more independent; yet quite a few seem to appreciate the way Norm tactfully takes charge and influences the buying decision—sometimes even makes it for them.

This kind of *Relationship* can give Norm added Motivational Selling

Leverage, as he moves the Fulcrum closer to the weight. And he does make a lot of sales.

Lew, on the other hand, builds an entirely different kind of *Relationship*. He is the serious, thoughtful, careful type; and he does a lot of listening and questioning. (Norm does most of the talking with his customers.) Lew's customers soon realize he is making a real effort to study them and to learn their preferences; and after trying on a few suits and discussing them with Lew, they realize that they are in the hands of a skilled and dedicated salesman who really wants to fit them out with a suit they will long enjoy wearing. Additionally, quite a few men come in with their wives, and it seems the wives are more likely to develop positive motivation with Lew than with Norm.

The kind of confidence Lew enjoys is very different from the kind Norm inspires. Lew's customers develop a sense of working cooperatively with him, as they progress toward a decision which, thanks to Lew's skillful guidance, they gladly make.

Second, *Benefits*. Norm talks benefits, but they are usually benefits that *he* sees and declares; and he is very good at selling them. But the benefits Lew sells almost sell themselves; that is, he works toward them collaboratively with the customer, guided by the person's physical characteristics and by all that he can learn of the person's tastes and preferences.

When Norm's customer shows the new purchase to his wife, he is likely to say: "The salesman told me this is the latest style; the chairman of General Motors wears one just like it." Lew's customer is likely to say: "Gee, this suit is really comfortable. I like it a lot, and I feel good in it."

Norm has his way of building up the benefits to lengthen the motivational Lever; but the Lever may be shorter after the customer gets home. Lew and his customer select the benefits together, and the benefits "stick." So the Motivational Selling Leverage that powers Lew's selling is likely to last.

Third, *Communication*. Most of Norm's selling *Communication* goes toward building himself up and toward building up benefits which later may not end up as benefits, in the customer's view. But Lew's selling *Communication* is devoted to finding out what will be the lasting *Benefits*, and helping the customer to realize what they are. Lew's customers remember what he said about the features they like; so the selling effect remains with them.

Norm uses "Forced Selling." He forces himself on the prospect as an expert and forces on the customer what he claims are benefits; his communication is aimed at forcing the customer to "see" the purchase in a certain way. It often works; it does produce positive motivation. But that, unfortunately, may not last.

Lew, on the other hand, uses "Natural Selling." His relationship with the prospect is easy, natural, and appropriate to the way he sells. When he sells the *Benefits*, the customer recognizes and accepts them as *Benefits*. And his *Communication* aims at determining what *Benefits* are valued by the customer, and clarifying and emphasizing these benefits.

"Natural Selling" and Motivational Selling Leverage together build the positive motivation that makes lasting sales.

Customer Values: The Basis of Positive Motivation

Example: Who Sold Jenny $63 Worth of Groceries?

Jenny Burton walks into her neighborhood supermarket, takes a shopping cart and a printed flyer that lists the day's specials, and pushes the cart from aisle to aisle, selecting various items until the cart is nearly full. She hasn't seen or talked to a single salesperson, but she has bought 17 different items; and she has run up a total of $63 in groceries.

Who sold those items to Jenny? How did Jenny get the positive motivation to buy them?

1. She was out of certain items that she uses regularly, or was running short of them.

2. She has some generalized needs, with some scope for discretionary choice. ("What shall we have for dinner tonight—spaghetti and meat balls, chili, or tuna and rice? Shall I buy Phoneyjoos for the kids, or should I try to get them to drink real fruit juice—cider, for instance? Should I get chocolate ice cream or fudge twirl?" etc.).

3. She is used to buying some items that have certain brand names.

4. She saw a few items that she hadn't counted on buying. One was something she uses occasionally; another looked like an improved version of a familiar item; still another was a novelty that she bought "on impulse"; and one was a special—at a very low price.

5. A range of factors influenced her, from remembering what a friend recommended, to an article in a magazine or a commercial on TV. In a few instances she selected items for which she held price-reducing coupons clipped from newspapers, magazines, and box-tops.

Jenny had many reasons for buying those 17 items; and she had many reasons for not buying other brands or for not buying other items in that well-stocked supermarket.

Jenny usually buys what she wants; and Jenny doesn't very often buy what she doesn't want. And when she wants something, that's because it has *value* for her.

The reasons why we want things, and buy them, are based upon our *values*. The price of an item is *not* the same as its value. The value is related in its importance to a particular individual under specific circumstances and at a particular time. For instance, the value of a glass of water to a person dying of thirst is different from the value of a glass of water to a person who has just had one, can have one free, any time, or who isn't thirsty. The value of an ounce of whiskey, to a teetotaler, is very different from its value to an alcoholic who "really needs a drink."

Of course, when it comes to selling, we are seldom faced with such extremes as these. But the principle illustrated is the same. People will still make their decisions to buy, or not to buy, on the basis of those positive values which influence *them*.

That brings us to our second basic axiom of selling:

AXIOM B: *Positive motivation is based on positive values.*

It follows, then, that the "art of selling" has to include dealing effectively with prospects' values. "Natural Selling" involves selling those benefits that the prospect will feel are related to his or her *positive values*. The more positive those values, and the more related the benefits are to those values, the more positive will be the motivation to buy. If the *Relationship* with the prospect helps the salesperson to learn the prospect's values and if the *Communication* does justice to the positive values of the benefits, then the Motivational Selling Leverage will make the sale (if it can be made).

When Jenny Burton bought those 17 items, she stopped at the butcher's counter to pick up some pre-packaged stew meat from the showcase, and she had a conversation with the butcher, which went like this:

Example: How to Sell Beef

JENNY: My parents and inlaws are coming for dinner next Sunday, so there'll be nine of us, altogether. I thought, maybe, a big steak. What do you think? A sirloin? A porterhouse? How big would it have to be? Six pounds? Eight? What do you think? I don't really want to spend all that money.

SAM THE BUTCHER: How about a nice, juicy rib roast? Everybody likes a good slice of roast beef! You could get by with, maybe, four, five pounds; and we have a special on it. Cost you a lot less than a steak.

JENNY: That sounds like a possibility.

SAM: Tell you what. Today's Tuesday. You'll be coming in again before Sunday. I'll pick you out a real, nice rib roast, and trim it down and have it ready for you. And I'll crack the bones so you can get them into a soup pot, after you

> devil what's left on them. Your husband will like working on that. And you know how to make Yorkshire Pudding. Goes great with roast beef!
>
> JENNY: OK! Do that. I'll pick it up Thursday.

Obviously, Sam is no slouch of a salesman. Of course, he had a lot to go on, but he learned right away where Jenny was "coming from"; and he built on values he knew would appeal to her. He came up with an answer to her need that satisfied her values. That was "Natural Selling," and the result was Jenny's positive motivation to buy the roast.

Sam's *Relationship* with Jenny is a good one for both of them. Jenny has confidence enough in Sam to tell him frankly about her needs, and Sam justifies and strengthens her confidence by being helpful—and by *not* taking advantage of her to build up the amount of the sale. Sam knows what *Benefits* to sell, and his *Communication* does the job in a simple, friendly, helpful way.

Sam has Motivational Selling Leverage working for him, and he's getting better all the time.

Of course, a supermarket is not the ideal setting to learn how to be a better salesperson. The aim there is to do away with personal selling. But the supermarket *is* a good place to learn how customers' values motivate them to buy. And Sam shows you how a salesperson can learn what the customer's positive values are and turn them into positive motivation to buy.

Of course, these are very simple examples of the principle of our Second Basic Axiom of selling. But it applies all the way along, to every selling situation there is.

Making Positive Motivation Work for You

Theoretically, a prospect may have what might be called 100 percent positive motivation to buy; but certainly, such situations are rare.

Example: 100 Percent Motivation

Suppose you were out alone in a boat, and it sank miles from shore. A small boat comes along, overcrowded with people. They have no room to take you aboard, but they offer to *sell* you a life preserver. You would probably have 100 percent positive motivation to buy it—at any price.

In such a situation, you would care about only one value, and that is what a life preserver could do for you. That is the benefit that makes the sale. Nobody has to sell it to you. The relationship with the vendor may be very unpleasant, but that doesn't affect your positive motivation to buy. The life preserver offers you a benefit that can save your life. That benefit sells itself.

Example: Competition for Urgent Needs

Now, suppose two boats come along, and each of them offers to sell you one life preserver. What would happen?

1. You'd have positive motivation to buy the life preserver that looked better to you—in better condition, safer, etc.
2. You'd probably have some positive motivation toward buying *both* life preservers.

Of course, you don't often find yourself in a position which forces that kind of positive motivation on you. But consider these other examples of positive motivation:

3. "I want a snow-thrower just like the one you sold my neighbor, Lew Gotch."
4. "I want the best golf clubs you have—better than the ones you sold my neighbor, Lew Gotch."
5. "I bought this electric shaver 11 years ago. It's worn out, unfortunately; but I want one exactly like it or one that is about the same."
6. "All my life I've wanted to own an original piece of artwork."

In each of these instances the customer's values have focused on certain benefits that provide positive motivation to buy a specific item. The customer's positive motivation centers on a *Benefit* that doesn't have to be sold; so neither *Relationship* nor *Communication* is a significant factor. Here are other situations:

7. "I always buy my shoes at Dango's; have for years. Alfredo, there, always knows just what I should be wearing."
8. "Congratulations on your new boutique, Laura, dear. I want to buy something from you—I don't care what—just for luck!"
9. "Certainly, sir, I'll be glad to buy a raffle ticket for your wife's favorite charity, and I'm sure all your other employees will be glad to buy them, too."

Such positive motivation is based on special *Relationships* between buyer and seller. The *Benefits* and the *Communication* have little to do with the positive motivation. The major factor in the decision to buy comes from the buyer's feeling or attitude toward or relations with the seller. The values which create the positive motivation arise from the buyer-seller relationship.

These are buying situations rather than selling situations, because the salespeople involved do not have to "sell the benefits," or create a relationship (since it already exists and it fosters a buying relationship). But that doesn't mean a salesperson should relax and just let such situations happen. Here are ways to be sure you do as well as possible in these situations.

1. Be alert: when you find positive motivation and pre-sold *Benefits* in a prospect, concentrate on those. Avoid distracting the prospect by offering anything less attractive.

2. Look for opportunities to create *Relationships* that will mean repeat business, with the customer depending more and more on your guidance and information. But remember: such *Relationship* must be based on confidence; you must show that you understand what *Benefits* appeal to the customer, and "sell" them in a way that will be justified by the customer's experience with the purchase. One disappointment can destroy a valuable relationship.

3. Be observant; "put two and two together." Learn what kind of people like what kind of product or service, and use such knowledge and experience in your selling. You can often "size people up" and make a good guess at what they will like. Showing that you know what they like is the best basis for making a sale.

How Communication Makes the Sale

We have discussed how positive motivation to buy makes selling easy. But even in such situations, exist, some *Communication* is necessary.

Example: The Overlooked Source

YOUR FRIEND: How do you like my new perfume?
YOU: Isn't that "Heaven Scent"?
YOUR FRIEND: That's right. How did you know?
YOU: I sell it.
YOUR FRIEND: You do? I didn't know that!
YOU: Well, I do. Where did you get it?
YOUR FRIEND: Oh, I just picked it up at Ludlum's.
YOU: Sure, they carry it, too. But so do I.
YOUR FRIEND: Gee, I'm really sorry. I didn't know. Better tell me what else you carry, so I'll know where to go for it.

Example: Another Overlooked Source

YOU: I see you're driving a new Phoenix sedan.
YOUR FRIEND: I sure am. How do you like it?
YOU: I'd like it better if you bought it from me.
YOUR FRIEND: What! Do you sell Phoenix?
YOU: Sure do, friend.
YOUR FRIEND: I didn't know that! I'm really sorry!
YOU: You have reason to be. I could have saved you a bundle.
YOUR FRIEND: I wish I'd known!

Of course, no one is going to buy something from you if they don't know you are selling it. Companies advertise their goods and services, but they don't necessarily advertise that *you* are selling those goods or services. That kind of advertising or promotion is usually left up to the individual salesperson, sales branch, or retail store.

Much advertising is aimed at communicating something besides information about the products or services for sale, and that something is a reminder of where it can be purchased. If you get to the point where you are beginning to think about buying something, you usually associate at least one source of supply with that potential purchase. But that may be a department store, supermarket, drugstore, or other retailer that you are used to buying from—not one especially associated with that particular product.

On the other hand, there are certain products (such as carpets, art, automobiles, TVs, stereos, videos, household appliances, etc.) that you are likely to associate with specialty stores or chains. You usually make that association because of the advertising you have seen in newspapers, magazines, and on TV.

The point of this is to suggest the difference between news of a change (a new source will handle a certain line of products, or an old source will now handle a new line of products); and a simple reminder (repeating that a well-known source offers a known line). Often, of course, the two effects are combined. But the aimed-at result is to *condition* you to associate a product or a service with an identified source, so that when you think of a product or service, you think of a particular source.

A salesperson should do all he or she can to develop the same kind of conditioning in as many prospects as possible, so that when they consider the purchase of something you can sell them, they will think of you. Your object should be to attract prospects who are presold on the *Benefits* (as discussed above) and who also have a special *Relationship* with you (as discussed in Chapter 6).

You can work toward such a goal by using *Communication* in two basic ways:

X: Depending on your own efforts at getting people to know about you and what you are selling;

Y: Depending on *Communication* by others—your satisfied customers —to tell about you and how well you serve them and how pleased they are in dealing with you.

The less you succeed with the second way (Y), the more you will need the first way (X); if you are successful the second way, the first way will take care of itself.

Talking a Prospect Into a Sale

There is another aspect of communicating to make a sale, which certainly needs to be discussed. A competent salesperson sometimes talks prospects into buying something they really do not want.

This kind of sale depends on benefits and relationship, but differs from the kinds of selling we have been discussing above. The communication is aimed at making the benefits, the relationship, or both, seem to the prospect as if they would provide values of some satisfaction to the prospect; but which turn out, after the purchase has been made, to be unsatisfactory and disappointing; so that the prospect regrets the purchase.

What is worse, some salespersons do this deliberately, regularly, habitually, or routinely.

At the beginning of this chapter you read: there is no such thing as a true sale without positive motivation. (Some people can be bull-dozed, hypnotized, seduced, misled, deceived, or otherwise pushed into a purchase they would not make otherwise, but it is still basically true that people will not, consciously and willingly, buy what they do not need, want, or like.)

Nevertheless, it is certainly a fact that some salespeople do make sales by overcoming the defenses of the prospects; leaving them in possession of something they do not want. Having made the purchase—or, rather, having fallen victim to a selling process which they submitted to—they now regret, and often even resent the experience and its result.

Some salespeople, as we know, even work for organizations which have developed, and require their salespersons to use, carefully planned methods of pressuring prospects into acquiescence: Some other salespersons use tactics that they have developed themselves; which may involve unethical forms of persuasion; and may even compel susceptible prospects to forget that they have the right to say no.

In this kind of selling you don't really want what you are buying; and you don't especially care about the person who is selling it; but the sales talk is so overwhelmingly high pressure that sometimes you just find it a lot easier—a relief—to say yes, instead of no.

Our second axiom of selling states, in effect, that people will buy only what they want. This is, of course, basically true. But there are all sorts of factors and influences that can make them want—or think they want—something that they did not want before, and will no longer want when those factors and influences are not at work on them.

There are four kinds of occasion when a person buys something that he or she does not really want:

1. The purchaser makes an error; that is, asks for and buys the wrong thing. But this is not a true sale, and it is not made by the "Whole

Customer." Some elements of the customer are cued (or miscued) attracted, stimulated, and the remainder of the customer is temporarily out of it until later.

2. The purchaser is unduly impressed by what he or she observes (the low price, the design, the color, the assumed usefulness, etc.) Later it turns out "the value is not there"; the design no longer looks right; the color changes in the light; it doesn't do what it was expected to do; etc.

3. The purchaser buys on the basis of assurances that turn out to be untrue and does not receive what he was told he was buying.

4. The purchaser is "bull-dozed" into buying by a bullying, forceful salesperson.

It may seem that sales made under conditions outlined in 1 and 2 are the customer's own fault, while those made in 3 and 4 are the responsibility of the salespersons involved. However, this would be a superficial view. Most such sales are the result of combinations of these categories, and 3 and 4 often contribute to the errors of 1 and 2.

So you see that, while it is basically true that people do not buy what they do not need, want or like, it *does* happen. And—unfortunately—some salespersons take advantages of opportunities to sell people what they do not need, want, or like.

This book is not about how to make sales by encouraging such errors. Rather, it is about selling that helps to eliminate such errors, selling that makes it as likely as possible that each purchase originates from genuine motivation and is based on values that are important to the customer.

Salespeople of the "hit and run" variety have no interest in building a continuing, helpful selling relationship, since they usually expect to make only a "one-shot" sale; they do not plan to be around when the disillusioned customer returns for his money back. The only relationship that interests them is that of inspiring the prospect with sufficient confidence in them, the product, and the terms to induce him to buy.

Such vendors usually offer products that appear to provide desirable benefits, but which turn out to be illusory. They characteristically conceal or down-play adverse features, and some utilize spurious testimonials and worthless guarantees to overcome the objections of the prospect.

They rely on communication—their kind of communication—to make the sale. In terms of Motivational Selling Leverage, they have to apply enough Force to overcome the lack of *real* benefits to the prospect and the dubious relationship in which they operate. They try to move the Fulcrum closer by improving the relationship, and they try to lengthen the Lever by selling the benefits; but in both these efforts their communication is deceptive, if not actually false.

Bright and capable salespersons who are facile communicators are often tempted to adopt such tactics. But if they are interested in an ongoing selling relationship, and if they take pride in their work and respect their profession, they will do well to avoid any questionable tactics and use their talents with an eye to the future, as well as to the present.

Using the Right Timing

There is a right time for everything. A good comedian is said to have *perfect timing*; that is, the pacing of his or her remarks, the pauses, hesitations, and the spacing contribute to the overall humorous effect of the words. A great orator also uses the best timing to make his ideas persuasive in their effect on the audience. A topnotch drill sergeant paces his commands so that they seem to have a specially compulsive character. The timing of a singer or conductor is crucial to their art. And the timing of a salesperson has to be right to bring about the greatest positive motivation in each prospect.

All of the examples above, however, deal with the timing of the elements of a set or relatively fixed or specific delivery which is repetitive; while in selling, the skillful use of such timing must be properly adapted to the individual prospect. There it can add greatly to the force of each different communication about the same benefits, supporting each different selling effort in a very substantial way.

But there is another, very important aspect of timing that can make a great deal of difference in the success of selling efforts. That is in the timing of different parts of the selling activities aimed at a prospect, in order to have these parts take effect at the most favorable moment, and to be more effective.

We all have been in situations where our arrival on the scene brought out such expressions as: "You couldn't have come at a better time!"; "So glad you came; we were just talking about you"; or "Just the person we were waiting for!"

Most of us have also lived through less welcoming situations, when we were met with such expressions as: "Sorry, I'm too busy to see you today!"; "It's just not convenient now!"; or "I can't possibly spare the time!"

Certainly, you should not arrive at prospects' offices when it is inconvenient—or impossible—for them to meet with you. If that happens you may embarrass them, or they may think you are a nuisance. At the least, you are distracting them from something they consider more urgent. Whatever their reaction, it will not help the relationship.

On the other hand, if you arrive at a time when you are expected and welcome, when the prospects are ready for you, they will be "tuned in" to you. To sell effectively, you need the attention of your prospect, and you need the opportunity to convert that attention into interest. If he is impatient, thinking about something else, feeling pressed for time, you are up against a barrier that can make it very difficult to do an effective job of selling.

Obviously, then, it should be worth your while to time—or at least try to time—your selling contacts so that they are likely to be well received; or—as a minimum—least likely to be unwelcome.

There are at least two aspects of good timing. One is to arrange matters so that selling contacts take place at times that are convenient to the prospect. The other has to do with preparing the prospect, or noting the development of his or her "readiness" to recognize and discuss a need or want, so that your selling "fits" what is in the prospect's mind.

Each prospect, and each selling situation, is different, so that no general rule will apply to all. But here are a few considerations that many experienced salespersons think are important.

Just before lunch is a bad time, because people who are hungry are less relaxed, less patient, less likely to be interested in anything outside their regular routines. Also, they may be very limited in time. This is especially true in isolated factories (or other establishments) where there is only one place to eat, and being late means standing in line too long.

Just after opening hours is likely to be a bad time, because people usually have work to do at their desks when they first reach them in the morning; they usually want to go over incoming items, and set their schedules for the day.

Late in the afternoon may be a bad time because people may be tired or feeling frustration over events of the day, and particularly near closing, when people may be thinking about getting away as early or as quickly as possible.

That leaves midmorning and after lunch through midafternoon as generally better times for selling activities.

Days of the week and of the month can also be critical in timing. Some prospects and customers are tied up on Mondays or Fridays because of the routines of their organizations; others may be involved in regularly scheduled activities on other days of the week or at certain times in the month. Some may have to take business trips on certain days of the week or month, and sales calls immediately preceding and following the days away may be untimely.

Many companies have stated periods of time assigned to certain functions (preparation of annual or monthly budgets, reports, plans and projections on sales, purchases, production, turnover, inventory, etc.), and during this time, people dislike being distracted from their obligations.

How often should you call on a prospect or regular customer? Many companies set regular calling schedules for their salespeople (once a week; once a month; once every six weeks, once a quarter, etc.). But this may not be suitable for some prospects. Alert salespersons will become aware of the best schedule for contracting certain individuals, and many sales managers will accept recommendations, based on such information, for exceptions to broadly aimed calling routines.

Keep in mind that good timing of contacts makes better *Relationships*, and good timing of *Communication* makes better selling through more positive motivation.

Judgment is another important consideration in timing. In a developing situation, for example, how soon should you get back to a prospect after making a sales proposal? If you do this too soon and he is not ready, it may cause a negative reaction; the prospect or customer may feel that he is being "pushed." But if he needs to be reminded and you do not do it, you could lose the sale. Use your judgment on such matters, and do not allow your own eagerness or impatience to influence your decision.

Using the Right Conditions for Positive Motivation

In any selling activity, there are some factors over which the salesperson has absolute control, many others over which the salesperson has some degree of control, and still others over which the salesperson normally has no control. Knowing what factors can be controlled and how to control them is one of the most important elements of effective selling.

However, there will always be some elements of the selling situation over which the salesperson has very little or no control; it is important that the salesperson identify such elements, realize or anticipate their effects, and take appropriate measures to offset any adverse influences they may have upon the sale.

Motivational Selling Leverage is intended to maximize the effectiveness of those factors over which the salesperson has considerable control, for developing positive motivation in the prospect. But it also provides the salesperson with a great deal of help in dealing with those factors over which he or she has little or no control.

Example: The Eager Prospect

Ned Wayburn is a skilled mechanic who has accumulated valuable experience in a small job-shop that undertakes special machining contracts for manufacturing companies. He and his wife (who also works) have saved some money, and for a long time he has planned to go into business for himself, opening a small job shop and doing the specialized work for customers who have promised him contracts.

He has studied his equipment requirements carefully and has decided that his major capital investment should be a machine tool that efficiently performs a set of operations. Though several companies produce such a machine, the Precision Tooling Group, Ltd. has recently announced an advanced model (the "Super-Precision Do-All") which Ned believes is ideally suited to his requirements. He has written to them, and they have sent

Malcolm DuBois, their sales and service representative for the region, to see him.

Malcolm finds Ned very eager to sign the order for delivery of the Super-Precision Do-All. So Malcolm finds that he really has no selling to do: Ned has sold himself on the *Benefit*. The only *Communicating* Malcolm has to do is to discuss a few administrative details. Then he takes the order.

Malcolm didn't have to do more because the prospect already had a high degree of positive motivation to buy the product.

The conditions faced by most salespeople are seldom like those in this example. Unfavorable conditions often have to be overcome before the salesperson develops enough positive motivation in the prospect to succeed in making a sale. (Chapter 6 provides several examples of this.)

What are the favorable and unfavorable conditions:

1. in the *Benefits* you can offer the prospect? The answer should be based on your knowledge of the prospect's needs as they apply to the product or service and your understanding of the background from which these needs arise.

2. in your *Relationship* with the prospect? The answer should include consideration of the accessibility and responsiveness of the prospect; the general tone and trend of interactions to date; the prospect's perception of the organization you represent; your relationship with others known to the prospect; and the potential value and effectiveness of any references you can offer.

3. in *Communicating* with the prospect? The answer to this should cover the provision of all information that can be of interest to the prospect in relating his needs to the *Benefits* you can make available, transmitted in the most appropriate form, and presented in such a way as to strengthen the *Relationship*.

Consideration of these three questions should result in identification of a number of conditions of obvious significance in making the desired sale to the prospect. The next step is to work on the more favorable conditions to maximize their positive effects and to provide a basis for countering any unfavorable conditions that have been identified.

Setting the Stage for Effective Selling

Everyone is affected by his or her environment.

That is a very simple statement, to which there is little dissent. And if that is true, surely it follows that an effective selling process calls for the salesperson to utilize the environment in such a way as to help develop a positive motivation to buy.

But there are two words in that statement that really control its significance. We must arrive at a full understanding of just what is meant by "*affected*"; and how much and in what way people are affected. Equally important is a full understanding of what is included in "the environment."

People behave in response to a "universe" of different factors, and these factors may be exerting various degrees of effect at any one time. All these factors can be divided into two categories: the internal and the external.

The internal factors include everything inside of us—ideas, memories, feelings, needs, sensory reactions, personal values, and the whole range of psychological functioning that goes on from moment to moment. The external factors include everything outside of us that enters into our conscious or unconscious perceptions.

Some experts divide the internal factors into two categories: the conscious processes of perceptions, sensations, reactions and "thought"; and the other factors of which we are unconscious, such as much of the functioning of our bodies, memories not called upon, and subconscious reactions and processes. (This second category of internal factors is sometimes called "the internal environment.")

Your prospect has his or her universe of internal factors and so do you; and the two universes are very different. What they have in common is only a very small part of each; but that modest overlap is the key to positive motivation of the prospect.

However, there are also all those external factors, the environmental factors which make up the sources of stimuli around you. When you and your prospect are together, you share the same environment—except that you are also part of the prospect's environment and the prospect is also part of yours.

If you are in the prospect's office, you (and whatever you bring with you) are the only unfamiliar elements in his or her environment. However, that situation changes when the prospect is with you in your office. Of course, the situation changes again when you and the prospect share other environments.

If the selling activity can be made more effective by a more sales-favorable environment, surely the salesperson should consider how this can be arranged. There are four major categories of environment:

1. Those environments most familiar to and wholly or largely controlled by the prospect. This usually means the prospect's own "space"—his or her office, or home, or other areas over which the prospect has authority or responsibility.

2. Those environments familiar to the prospect, but not special to or in any way controlled by the prospect. This would include any areas controlled by the prospect's employer, such as plant or office areas, branches, or warehouses, or other premises operated by the prospect's employer, but where the prospect does not have direct authority or responsibilities.

3. Places or areas where the salesperson has a "host" role. This includes the salesperson's "home grounds"—office, home, car, employer's plants, company plane, etc.; also clubs and other facilities where the salesperson is providing entertainment, demonstration, training, or other sales-related activity. It could include restaurants, hotels, and conference centers where the salesperson has a special status.

4. Neutral territory: areas or places where neither the prospect nor the salesperson has any regular formal or informal connection. This includes restaurants, hotels, and transportation facilities.

It is clear that in all of these environments, the salesperson himself is the most important element over which he has any control. Even if the salesperson has almost complete control of the environment, as when he entertains the prospect at his own home, the importance of the salesperson himself, as a part of the environment affecting the prospect, does not lessen. In fact, it may be enhanced as the prospect observes the salesperson as a Whole Person.

Changing the prospect's environment from (a) or (b) to (c) not only gives the salesperson opportunities to improve the *Relationship* but also allows him or her to learn about the value to the prospect of the *Benefits* that the salesperson can offer.

Changing the prospect's environment from (a) or (b) to (d) gives the salesperson an opportunity to develop the *Relationship* on a more personal basis. This can lead to helpful insights about the values that are important to the prospect and how best to *Communicate* with the prospect about them.

But the salesperson must be aware when starting a *Relationship* with a prospect in environment 1) that he is the only part of that environment which can develop positive motivation in the prospect. There is usually not much use relying on what could happen in environments (3) and (4) if the salesperson generates too little positive motivation in environment (1).

RELATIONSHIP + BENEFITS +   COMMUNICATION→EFFECT

Bare Relationship	Benefits dubious or not recognized	Communication not geared to appropriate benefits	Not a chance
Working Relationship	Benefits more or less comparable to competition	Communication not well geared to prospect's needs	Maybe
Good Selling Relationship	Benefits most desired by prospect	Communication presents benefits that fit prospect's needs	Positive motivation to buy!

How Natural Selling Creates Positive Motivation

We have seen that the prospect can develop a positive motivation to buy—without the intervention of a salesperson—when he learns about the benefits and realizes that these benefits meet his needs. But we know that most of the time the prospect does not learn this on his own, so it is necessary to "sell the benefits." We also know that it is up to the salesperson to sell the benefits in the most effective way possible, using the *Communication* that is suited to the particular prospect and to the *Benefits* that are of value to him.

We also know that our *Relationship* with the prospect is important—not only to develop confidence in the truth of what we say, and in our own real interest in bringing about a sale that will be satisfactory to the prospect—but also to help us learn about the prospect's wants and needs; how the prospect perceives the product or service we offer, and the *Benefits* it can bring; whether such perception is adequate; if the perception can be enhanced and made more favorable; and, if so, how this can be done.

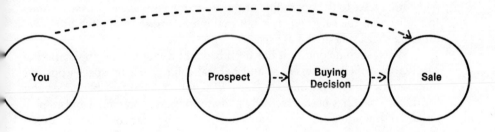

You want the Prospect to make a decision to buy—from you.

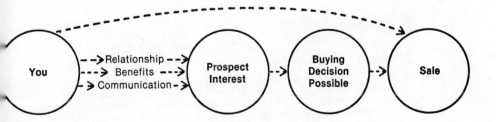

You should develop a favorable selling *Relationship*; identify the *Benefits* that will best satisfy the prospect's needs and wants; and *Communicate* these in terms of the prospect's values.

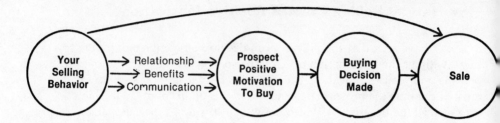

If the *Relationship* is satisfactory and the appropriate *Benefits* are *Communicated* effectively, you create a positive motivation to buy. A favorable buying decision will follow, and you will make the sale—if the other Essential Conditions (see Chapter 8) are met.

When you sell the *Benefits* from your perception of the prospect's needs, you move from formula and "scatter-shot" sales talk to the level of natural selling—selling that is highly adapted (natural) to the individuality of the prospect and to the potential values to be derived by the prospect from the product or service you are offering.

Natural selling arises from a favorable *Relationship* with the prospect and contributes to the upgrading of that *Relationship,* as the prospect comes to realize that the salesperson is not making an impersonal pitch but is addressing the needs of the prospect.

When such a condition has been brought about by the application of Motivational Selling Leverage and natural selling, the prospect's positive motivation to buy is maximized. Every *Benefit* that could possibly have value for the prospect has been effectively and appropriately presented and emphasized. All the potential applications of the *Benefits* that could be of interest to the prospect have been clearly and forcefully shown. The benefits have been sold in terms of their relevance to the prospect's situation and in ways that emphasize the advantages to *this* prospect.

Such a selling process, of course, is likely to result in an order. But if it does not, the salesperson is in a position to learn why. And the possible reasons are likely to be among these:

1. The price is too high.
2. The terms are not acceptable.
3. Delivery is unsatisfactory.
4. There is a competitive situation
   a. in which the final proposal has not been submitted;
   b. which is less costly;
   c. which looks better in terms of benefits.
5. There is a problem of *Relationship:*
   a. a competitor has an inside track;
   b. the prospect has doubts about or an aversion to the salesperson or to his company, product, or service;

   c. the prospect's company has some special *Relationship* with a competitor.

6. There is a misunderstanding or failure of *Communication*.

7. The prospect is not serious. (He or she may be "just shopping around," or he or she may have had intentions to buy at first but changed plans.)

8. Change of personnel; prospect now represented by entirely different person with different values, priorities, authority, etc.

For guidance in handling such situations, see Chapter 8.

★★ 6 ★★

Selling Leverage: New Ways to Pitch Benefits to Targeted Prospects

How the Selling Relationship Differs from the Personal Relationship

Remember that a good selling *Relationship* is a *Relationship* between you and a prospect or customer that is conducive to a sale or sales, that will be in the interests of both vendor and purchaser.

Anything which contributes in a positive way to a sale is also likely to contribute to a good selling *Relationship*. Many excellent selling *Relationships* have been created on the basis of little more than the prospect's recognition that the information provided by a salesperson is accurate, reliable, and helpful.

It should be clear that a selling *Relationship* and a personal relationship are quite different, though salespeople and prospects often have both kinds of relationship. However, a personal relationship does not constitute a selling *Relationship*. The following example illustrates this.

Example: A Personal Relationship That Does Not Make a Sale

Nat Osborne, manager of the Insurance Department of Invincible Oil, a large energy corporation, is in charge of insurance purchasing. His daughter Natalie has taken a position with the insurance brokerage firm of Skelly and Bloom, has completed her training as a salesperson of group insurance policies, and has been assigned a list of prospects that includes her father.

This is her first business call, and both father and daughter are trying to be business-like. She goes into her prepared pitch for the hospital-medical-surgical-dental coverage of Invincible's 30,000 employees. She makes a good presentation, and ends by handing Nat a written proposal covering the bid for Invincible's business.

Nat glances at the document, smiling with pride at his daughter's performance.

"Well, Miss Osborne," he begins, "if you were any other youngster just beginning your career in this field and you started out as well as that, I'd say you have a bright future ahead of you. But since you are my daughter, I'll tell you a few things it may do you good to know, and that I probably wouldn't bother to tell anyone else in your place.

"First of all, Skelly and Bloom should never have sent you here, and they know it! Apart from the fact that it might have embarrassed both of us, they've had a very good representative, Vera Gordon, calling on me for quite a few years. She knows the picture here, and she knows all the reasons why we haven't done business with your firm. One of the reasons is that most of our claims originate in Louisiana and Wyoming, and you have no offices nearer than Atlanta and Chicago. Another reason is that we are now dealing—quite satisfactorily—with Infallible Assurance. We deal with them directly; no brokerage involved; therefore, the price is right. Finally, we just happen to own most of Infallible, so of course they have the inside track.

"But don't give up hope. Infallible doesn't write life insurance; so we shop around for our Group Life and Key Man policies, which you haven't mentioned. But, for us, buying insurance is a completely objective decision, based on how we value the service we expect against the cost we have to pay. Getting our business takes a lot of close, tedious figuring. When the time comes to present the figures, what counts is that the person who presents them can handle all the complications we throw at him or her. If Skelly and Bloom want you to make that presentation—daughter or no daughter—you'd better be ready!"

Natalie has a very good relationship with her father, but it is purely a personal relationship. It got her some information and some advice (personal relationships can do that very well); but it didn't get her a sale.

Not many salespersons handle sales as complicated as group insurance policies for large corporations, but the principle that Nat explained to his daughter is likely to apply to the selling of almost any product or service.

The effect of a personal relationship on selling is illustrated in the following example.

Example: A Personal Relationship That Makes a Sale

Mrs. Norma Bray is an elderly widow, wealthy, and almost alone in the world. She has no children; her nearest living relative is her nephew, Hugo, who is in the real estate business. He is very busy trying to make a

living and to pay for all the fun he likes to have in the evenings. He is a
bachelor, and he isn't as attentive to his aunt as she would like. Now she
has telephoned Hugo's office and has left a message directing him to come
to her immediately after office hours. She adds that "this is a business matter."

Hugo cannot disregard such a summons from his only wealthy relative. He rings the doorbell of her apartment promptly at 5:30. After the greet-
ings, Mrs. Bray comes to the point.

"Hugo, you know the new deluxe condominiums on Sutton Plaza? My
friend Mimi Bedford has bought one, and I was over there after lunch to
see it. Well, I've decided to buy one like it—it's apartment 21A. My lease
here expires this fall, and I'd move right in. Somebody will get the commission, and it might as well be you. So go and buy it for me right away, before
it's sold to someone else. I want the one on the 21st floor, on the side that
has a view of the river."

Hugo murmurs agreement. Mrs. Bray continues.

"Now, Hugo, remember! You didn't sell me this condo. I decided to
buy it. So don't get the idea that you really earned the commission. Actually, I'm giving the commission to you because you're my nephew—even if
I hardly ever see you. You don't really deserve it, the way you neglect your
poor old aunt."

Hugo expresses profound gratitude and promises to do better.

Mrs. Norma Bray was absolutely right: her relationship with Hugo was
not a selling *Relationship*. Technically, he is selling her the condo, but it is
their personal relationship that led to the sale. No true selling *Relationship*
was involved.

It is important to remember that many selling situations involve both
a selling *Relationship* and a personal relationship, and it is important to know
which of these relationships you are creating or reinforcing. You may have
a close personal relationship without its doing a thing toward a selling *Relationship*, and you may develop an effective selling *Relationship* without much
of a personal relationship. Don't mistake one for the other, and always be
sure which one can help you sell.

How to Start the Right Relationship

The best way to go about almost anything is to make a good beginning, and that is certainly true when it comes to selling. Making a good start
in selling means starting with the best possible relationship.

There have been times when demand for a product exceeded supply
and people selling the product have been hard pressed to meet the demand.
There also are times when a certain product becomes so popular that it does
not have to be sold—the orders just keep coming in. But such situations are
unusual and do not last long. By and large, products and services have to
be sold and the salesperson has to develop the right kind of *Relationship*
with prospects.

There are two sides to the way anyone perceives a *Relationship:* the objective and the subjective. A salesperson meeting a prospect for the first time usually does not know and certainly cannot control the subjective factors influencing a prospect. However, there are four major objectives that a prospect is faced with, and very likely to be influenced by, when prospect and salesperson meet for the first time. These are:

1. The salesperson as a person.
2. The salesperson as a salesperson.
3. The product or service offered by the salesperson.
4. The firm or organization represented by the salesperson.

The prospect may have feelings, or opinions about #3 and #4 in advance of the meeting, perhaps derived from observation, information, or experience dating back in time. If so, certain impressions will be formed when the appointment is first made (or when the prospect sees the salesperson's card). A certain impression is also formed in advance of the meeting by the way the appointment is made, by the way the caller is announced, by the appearance of the salesperson's card, and by the first glimpse of the salesperson, before a word is spoken.

Obviously, the more favorable the impressions created before salesperson and prospect speak to one another, the better; but what can be done to bring this about? What cannot be helped? And what can the salesperson do to create a favorable opening impression?

To begin with, let us agree that most prospects have their own sets of values that color their first impression of a salesperson. We usually can do little or nothing about such values in advance of a meeting, but there are some values we can anticipate or assume. Among such values are those concerning the prospect's interests, time, and energy. We may reasonably except that most prospects will form an unfavorable impression of a salesperson who they believe will try to sell them something they have little or no interest in and who will take up too much of their time. On the other hand, they may look forward to seeing a salesperson who can tell them about something in which they have an interest and who will not take too long to do it.

But there are a number of ways in which a salesperson may offend the prospect. While some prospects care little about any aspect of a salesperson's call except what he or she is offering and the price, others care about personal matters that may affect the *Relationship.* For instance, an article of dress such as a necktie or piece of jewelry may cause a good or bad impression. Some prospects resent having a salesperson call them by their first names, before an appropriate level of relationship has developed. Some prospects dislike people who chew gum (especially with their mouths open), people who lounge in their chairs, people who light up a cigarette without asking permission, etc. Salespeople who—knowingly or unknowingly—offend their prospects in such ways are "shooting themselves in the foot."

Thus, from the moment planning for the meeting begins, the salesperson should be thinking not only about matters of interest to the prospect but also of making clear to the prospect that he will discuss only such matters. Furthermore, it is desirable for the salesperson to convey the impression that he is time-conscious and succinct.

The salesperson should begin with available information about the prospect before the appointment is made. In making the appointment, these tactics may be helpful.

1. Your company may be large and prestigious, but the prospect may not know what it can offer him. It is often useful therefore, to identify the division, subsidiary, or other area of your company that you represent.

2. Your firm may market a variety of products or services, which the prospect may not know about and which may be of interest to him. It is often helpful to identify early in the contact the products or services you wish to discuss.

3. It may be constructive to make reference to any prior relationship: a salesperson from your company who used to call on the prospect, purchases made at some prior period, sales to other components (plants, branches, etc.) of the prospect's organization.

4. In making an appointment, so far as possible, leave the date and time of day up to the prospect.

5. If you talk to the prospect's secretary, you can often learn the best time to see the prospect. If you are traveling, and your time in the prospect's area is limited, be as flexible as possible.

6. It is sometimes helpful to say something like: "If you are pressed for time, I can give you the basic information in less than ten minutes, and leave some material with you to look at when you can."

7. Your calling card should suggest the "image" you want to be associated with you: direct and to the point; not cluttered with fancy decorations and unnecessary print.

8. Books have been written about how salespersons should dress. Of course, situations and conditions (not to mention climates, seasons, cultural and regional and local customs and fashions, etc.) should be considered. But there is no question that clothing and other elements of the salesperson's personal appearance do affect the impression made upon the prospect. The salesperson should certainly bear in mind the prospect's most probable values, preferences, expectations, and standards in order to make a favorable impression on the prospect.

How to Use Entertainment and Gifts

There can be little doubt that entertainment has helped to build some *Relationships*, and has led to the passing, from prospect to salesperson, of information useful in promoting sales. It has also influenced the positive motivation to buy—often by contributing to the winning of support among those involved in organizational buying decisions.

The only real advantage that can be gained by spending money on a prospect (assuming he or she is honest, and no bribery or other unethical inducement is involved) is in building up the personal relationship. If that is done in a positive, constructive way, it can indeed contribute to the power of your Motivational Selling Leverage.

Entertainment can also provide better opportunities for learning about the prospect's needs, wants, and values; and the factors involved in arriving at a buying decision.

The more you can learn about what the prospect needs or likes about what you are selling, the better supplied you are with the information you need to "sell the benefits" the prospect values—and to develop the positive motivations that will make the sale. The more capable you are of building those positive motivations, the more advantages you have in using effectively what you can learn about the prospect's needs, wants, and likes. Perhaps the best use you can make of entertainment is to derive the information you need.

Prospects differ greatly among themselves in what they want, expect, or will accept from salespersons—in terms of relationships, entertainment, gifts, or any other "freebies." Here are a few examples of different kinds of prospects, and the kinds of *Relationships* they are most likely to accept when it comes to entertainment and gifts.

Example: The Very Conservative Prospect

Lester Pilkington is a middle-aged family man. For 16 years, he has been the purchasing agent for chemicals and fillers for Plastics International. Occasionally, he accepts a luncheon from a salesperson with whom he wants to discuss something at greater length; but he turns down the pretentious, expensive places and insists on modest, local eateries. He won't have a drink (not even beer or wine) and sometimes even insists on paying his share of the bill. The only time Lester was ever known to accept a gift was when a salesman he had dealt with for years brought him a catcher's mitt for his son, a Little Leaguer. Lester hesitated quite a while before he finally accepted that gift.

Lester buys fairly and objectively. He tells you what he wants, and when, and how; and it is up to you to come nearest to giving him what he wants at the right price. Your *Relationship* with Lester is quite impersonal; but you can have a good working and selling *Relationship* with him. It will not be a personal relationship, and there is little you can do to "warm it up."

There are many conservative prospects like Lester Pilkington, and salespeople can have a satisfying and rewarding *Relationship* with them, selling to them quite effectively, without ever getting on a personal or intimate basis.

Example: Some Good Selling Relationships Need Little More

Sam North is a purchasing agent for Summit Retailers; he buys men's clothing for their seven stores. Sam knows that it is good business to build up a sound *Relationship* with suppliers, and that having good *Relationships* with their representatives is advantageous to him and to his employer. He has identified three to eight qualified suppliers for each class of merchandise that he buys, and he likes to give at least some business to each of them, to keep the *Relationship* going. If a supplier offers one or more "hot" items, of course, he will buy all that the stores can sell; and if one of his regular supplier's offerings are below his standard, he will try to do something constructive about it.

"I don't think your colors are right," he may say to a necktie salesperson. "I can't take more than a couple of gross, assorted. But maybe we can do some business next month on scarves. Bring me a few samples in solid, conservative colors and maybe a few patterns on the conventional side— nothing too bright or wild. We see a good possibility for the fall."

Or: "We seem to be overstocked on zip-in-lining raincoats like these. But I'd be interested in suburban coats—especially lighter weight. Maybe some corduroy? Bring me a few samples—and watch your prices. Remember we have to compete with Valley and Grover's. I expect better quality than Garvin's discounter line, and I want it to show. Bring me what I want, priced to compete with Garvin's superior line, and I might order up to 20 gross."

Sam will go out to lunch or dinner once in a while but only with salespeople he is doing business with regularly. He never picks the place, and if they start for one of the expensive restaurants, he will suggest that a quiet place where they can talk would be better. Sam has a rigid rule: *no* presents.

You cannot build a *Relationship* with Sam by offering entertainment or gifts; but if Sam creates the *Relationship* by making you a regular supplier, the modest entertainment he will accept may help to build an effective selling *Relationship*.

Of course, there are other prospects who will accept a lot more than Lester Pilkington or Sam North; and with whom it is possible to build a much closer selling *Relationship*, on a sound basis.

Example: A Well-Lubricated Relationship

Grover Stennis owns a small company that produces cartons. He purchases all the materials used in his plant, much of it paperboard. Many companies want to sell him the stock he uses, and he might be able to save by shopping around. But Grover believes in the importance of long-term reliability. He wants to deal with a supplier he can depend on, as his customers have learned to depend on him. So he does business with Glenn Graham, who sells for Burke, Ltd.

Grover has been ordering paperboard from Glenn for years. It is a satisfactory arrangement for both of them, and they are good friends. They and their wives often dine together in the best places, and Glenn always picks up the check. Sometimes, Glenn buys tickets for the theatre or for a major sporting event, and he usually provides a chauffeured limousine for such occasions. Several times the two couples have taken deluxe trips together—all at the expense of Glenn's company.

Grover would probably buy from Glenn without all that lush entertainment. But Glenn's company provides him with a liberal expense account, and the business Glenn gets from Grover justifies what Glenn spends on him. So, between the two of them, there is a kind of unspoken agreement to enjoy the situation on the basis of "why not?"

The lesson we can learn from this example is this: When the business relationship between salesperson and customer is satisfactory to both and the two individuals are personally compatible, they might very well have a friendly personal relationship; entertainment and gifts alone, then, would not make the sale, but they might "lubricate" the *Relationship* and thus facilitate the sales.

There is often a point in a selling *Relationship* when a transition takes place, from impersonal business interacting to the beginning of a recognition by both prospect and salesperson of the other as a "Whole Person." Often, this point is marked by the prospect's acceptance of an invitation to leave his/her own "territory" and partake of a meal with the salesperson.

Example: The Turning Point

Gwen Parsons sells "office temporaries" for Personpower, Inc. She is calling on Lydia Prentice, the officer manager of Grigsby Wholesalers, a company that often uses temporary help to handle fluctuations in business volume.

Gwen is only 23, and a year out of Wellesley College. Lydia is 47 and "came up the hard way," going to work as soon as she finished high school. In addition, Gwen is attractive, and fashionably dressed; Lydia is plain, and a bit of a frump.

Lydia is called on by salespeople for all the organizations offering temporary help, and she feels most comfortable with middle-aged women who have backgrounds like her own. She does not feel comfortable with Gwen and has never done business with Personpower. This is Gwen's third call on Lydia, and she is explaining the availability of computer programmers, shipping clerks, porters, and other categories of nonsecretarial personnel. Although Lydia listens closely, she has no intention of doing business with Personpower, but she is thinking of asking her regular suppliers about some of the services Gwen is discussing.

Gwen is quite aware that Lydia is "cold" to her and that she is not "breaking through." So she decides on a new tactic.

"You seem interested in the possibility of using some of these special categories of personnel, Ms. Prentice," she says. "What could be very helpful to you is a visit to the Graber Company. They're big wholesalers, operating the way you do, but they handle different lines, so they're not competitors. I'd like you to meet their office manager, Ben Firkin. You'd like him, and I'm sure he'd be glad to meet you. You'd both have a lot to talk about. If you'd like, you can make it a lunch date, too. I'll pick you up here about 11 and take you to Graber. After an hour or so we can lunch nearby—say at the Superb. If you like shad roe, it's just coming in, and theirs is the best! Just tell me what day would be best for you and I'll check with Ben Firkin."

Lydia seldom gets out of the office for lunch, and she has been "brown-bagging" for years; she has heard of but has never been to the Superb, and would really love to try shad roe. She also knows the Graber Company has a very "advanced" operation, which it would benefit her to see. So she accepts.

That marks the turning point in the *Relationship* between Gwen and Lydia and the beginning of a productive *Relationship.*

In the Graber office and at lunch, Lydia talks and behaves very differently from how she does in her office. She sees that Gwen, as hostess at luncheon, is charming and pleasant.

Gwen's successful tactic definitely moved the Fulcrum much closer to the Weight—for much better Motivational Selling Leverage.

How **Not** to Use Entertainment and Gifts

Selling is a business, of course; and when people pay good money for products or services, they know that they are involved in a business transaction. Some people like to do business with "friends," and many long-standing and valued friendships have grown out of what started as a business *Relationship.* But many people prefer for various reasons to keep their personal relationships and their business relationships apart. Under such circumstances, any offer of entertainment or gifts would probably have a negative effect.

Many corporations and government agencies have rules forbidding or limiting what their officers or employees may accept; many organizations exercise various controls over what their representatives may offer.

Officials have gone to jail over the acceptance of "favors," and many purchasing agents have been fired for receiving what their managements considered "undue" or "excessive" personal benefits from vendors. For such reasons, many professional buyers acting for firms, corporations, or other organizations (including government agencies) believe it best to keep "some distance" between themselves and the salespeople who call on them.

Some prospects and customers do not care for three-martini lunches, fancy dinners, theatre, nightclubs, or even fishing or hunting trips. Many buyers are teetotalers, non-smokers, vulnerable to seasickness, and hate "blood-sports." Of course, there are others who accept (and may even expect) favors, but they usually regard such treatment as their due, do not especially appreciate it, and feel no particular obligation to anyone because of it.

On the other hand, there can also be little doubt that many hard-boiled businesspeople—purchasing agents, buyers, executives, staff experts and others, among them—not only accept costly entertainment and gifts, but also accept them from different salespersons who are in competition with one another. This is done without any sense of obligation to anyone; and with no meaningful enhancement of any relationship involved, other than that which results from such impressions as: "Jan knows the best restaurants"; or "Tom got seats to the opening game of the World Series when nobody else could"; or "Joe obviously has a much bigger expense account than Pete or Jean."

Example: Letting the Good Times Roll

Ernie Manship is a buyer for Supercity Stores. About fifty he is a hearty, red-faced sports fan and gourmet. He loves a "good time," and he counts on certain cooperative salespeople to provide it. Ernie has a regular routine: he lets the salespeople know the restaurant, the theatre or sporting event, and the nightclub of his choice, and they make the reservations. Most of the salespeople enjoy these expensive indulgences (which they could not afford themselves, but which their expense accounts make available).

Ernie is particularly on the take around Christmas time. He receives cases of fine vintage wines, expensive cameras, top-quality stereo components, and other rather costly gifts. Some of these come at Ernie's request (or broad hints) from salespeople who have received substantial orders; others come from salespeople who only hope for orders.

All this finagling has not escaped the notice of Ernie's superiors, who are beginning to question the professional objectivity of Ernie's buying decisions. One day they will probably "put two and two together" and Ernie will no longer be working for Supercity Stores. In addition, marketing and sales executives of several supplier companies have become concerned about their cost of sales to Supercity Stores. Some of their salespeople spend inordinately large amounts of their expense accounts on Ernie.

Computer analyses show that good selling results do not always correlate with big spending on entertainment and gifts. The value of certain salespeople to their organizations is being reconsidered in light of their costs of selling. Undoubtedly, some of them will turn out to be not very profitable representatives.

Some situations are even more extreme and present problems that extend to senior management levels, as the following example illustrates.

Example: Expecting Too Much

Alfred Nesbit is president of Nesbit Furniture, a substantial retailer in a big city in the Southwest, which sells a high volume of high-priced lines. One of the lines he carries in his city on an exclusive basis is that of Garson-Dikovsky, manufacturers of a line that is doing very well in fashionable stores around the country. Nesbit sells about 15 to 20 percent of Garson-Dikovsky's total output. Consequently, he feels that he is very important to them.

Garson-Dikovsky's representative, Pat Greer, calls on Nesbit regularly, but Nesbit figures that an important customer like himself should deal with the chairman, Louis Garson, or the president, Hank Dikovsky, and that they should call on him and, at least occasionally, entertain him and Mrs. Nesbit; and when he comes to Atlanta, where Garson-Dikovsky has its headquarters, he wants a suite in the best hotel in town.

So far, Garson and Dikovsky have gone along with Nesbit's expectations. But each time, they wonder if it's worth it; if they should say no to Nesbit's demands—and what would happen if they did. Greer has plans to find out if other major suppliers to Nesbit are providing him with the same kind of perquisites; and he has been told to explore the possibility of switching to another retailer in Nesbit's city.

Nesbit believes he has a right to all he can get, and that Garson-Dikovsky owes it to him for carrying their line. Garson, Dikovsky, and Greer do not like to sell that way and will eventually balk. Their idea is to plan so that when they do make a change, Nesbit, and not themselves, will lose by it.

Entertainment and gifts for a prospect add to the cost of sales, as well as take up the attention, time, and energy of the salesperson. The relationship to which all this "extra" has been directed should be subjected to at least this question: Could anything like this relationship exist, between the individuals involved, on any other basis? Or is it wholly dependent upon the entertainment provided? Even if the answer is that the relationship "is a natural," there is another, very important question that should be asked. The true test of whether or not all this "extra" is worthwhile is not whether it builds some kind of *Relationship*. It is this: Does it really help to make the sale?

Being Helpful

Example: How Dave Dingell Missed His Cues with Dr. Portham

Dave Dingell is a "detailer" for Cosmic Pharmaceuticals. His assignment consists of a panel—a list of about 600 doctors in his area, who specialize in internal medicine, especially in heart disease. Dave is theoretically supposed to call on each of these doctors once in every six-week cycle, which works out to 100 per week, or an average of 20 per day. But that is just about impossible; any day Dave can actually get to see 12 or even 10 is an exceptionally productive day.

Detailers have a special kind of selling job. They call on doctors who do not buy, but may prescribe. The doctor's patients will buy if—and what—the doctor prescribes; and they can buy it only from a pharmacy that happens to stock it or is willing to order it from a supply warehouse. The function of the detailer is to motivate the doctor to prescribe the formulations of the detailer's company; this is not easy to do.

The doctors to be called on—those listed on the panel—are the big prescribers—the best prospects for a lot of prescriptions. By that same token, they are busy and (usually) prosperous. During the doctor's office hours his waiting room is full of people waiting for him to see them; most of them have appointments. There is a receptionist who knows all the detailers who make regular calls (there are many of them, from many companies—often with competitive products). The receptionist knows which ones the doctor wants to see and which ones he doesn't want to see.

Dave is calling on Dr. Kay Portham, whom he has been unable to see the last two times he has called here; so it has been 4½ months since he last spoke with Dr. Portham. The nurse-receptionist has told Dave to wait.

After about 10 minutes, Dr. Portham appears in the entrance to the hall that leads to her office. She beckons to Dave, who joins her there.

"Well, Mr. Dingell, is there anything new from Cosmic that I ought to know?"

"Well, yes, Dr. Portham, there is—a matter that should be of great interest to you. It is about the side-effects from some of the popular prescriptions for treating hypertension."

"Always interested in that. Let's have it."

"Well, doctor, tests at Mt. Sinai Hospital in Dayton show that Downgo—that's the German import from Kreutzer—can cause nausea and headaches; but our Lowtense is free of those side-effects. Here's a reprint from the Northeast Journal of Medicine that gives the whole story. And here are some samples of Lowtense."

"Well, Mr. Dingell, I know about the side-effects of Downgo, and I know about the side-effects of Lowtense—depression and, in some cases, impotence. You can give the samples to Nancy."

Then Dr. Portham mutters a perfunctory "thanks" as she turns away, leaving Dave with the realization that he has wasted the call.

Dave had six weeks before he was required to see Dr. Portham again. During this time, he talked to his supervisor and to a detailer that used to call on Dr. Portham, and he studied all the materials his company could provide about the products that would be of possible interest to Dr. Portham. He also put together an approach he thought would work better than the others he had tried. And he even went over it with Cosmic's staff trainer and his supervisor.

When he reached the doctor's office he gave the receptionist a note for Dr. Portham. It read:

"Dear Dr. Portham: Knowing your interest in the side-effects of the various prescription drugs available for the treatment of hypertension, I have prepared a comprehensive list showing the potential side-effects of each and their potential seriousness.

"You will note that our Lowtense, as you stated, does sometimes induce side-effects of nausea and impotence. However, it is clear from extensive clinical evidence (the references are attached) that the side-effect of nausea has been noted only three times—in each case in patients who were also suffering from other nausea-inducing ailments. The side-effect of impotence was actually noted only once, in the case of a patient hospitalized for acute alcoholism and exhaustion. Therefore, there is no clinical indication that Lowtense will exert such undesirable side-effects in patients who are free of these secondary afflictions.

"If there is anything further along these lines that it would be helpful for you to know, it will be my pleasure to secure the information for you. Sincerely, Dave Dingell."

Nancy's intercom buzzed; Dr. Portham wanted to see Dave. In the doctor's office, comfortably seated and feeling welcome, Dave received the doctor's thanks for the note—plus a few follow-up questions, to which Dave promised answers from Cosmic Research on his next call.

As Dave left, Dr. Portham thanked him again and added: "Please drop off a few more samples of Lowtense with my receptionist."

Providing Helpful Services

Example: The Opening Wedge

SALESPERSON BEN: In your electric arc furnaces, Rick, how many pounds of graphite electrode do you use per ton of steel produced over a typical month?

MILL SUPERINTENDENT RICK: Last month we averaged 28 pounds of graphite per ton of steel.

BEN: How much of that 28 pounds of graphite do you figure was wasted?

RICK: About 12 pounds per ton of steel is poured for just the erosion of the arc. The rest is wasted.

BEN: That's 16 pounds of graphite down the drain.

RICK: Listen, Ben. You know we're buying Royal electrodes, with Imperial as a back-up supplier. So we don't need a third source of supply.

BEN: Rick, we can show you how much graphite you're wasting and what you can do to cut down on that waste, we can show your people on the shop floor who handle the electrodes what they are doing wrong.

RICK: We've never done anything like that. How is this program scheduled?

BEN: Two-hour sessions for each shift—about a month apart; three sessions over three months. You have to bring them off the floor to a quiet place that's like a classroom. We'll put on the program—at no charge to you.

RICK: Who will put on the program?

BEN: We have an expert who developed this program and who has put in a lot of time studying electric furnace steel mills. Your men should learn a lot from the sessions. And I'll be there, Rick, in case anybody has questions for me.

Rick's acceptance of this innovative service led to an active *Relationship* which was very profitable to Ben's company.

How Benjamin Franklin Helped Lucy Novak

Example: Building Relationship By Asking a Favor

Lucy Novak sells kitchen appliances for Imperial Products Corporation. The biggest prospect in her territory is the headquarters buying office of Global Retailers, Inc., a major chain of department stores. Global stores carry six lines of kitchen appliances, but the Imperial line was not one of them. The Global buyer is Jenny Snote, who had been giving Lucy a difficult time because she thought Global didn't need anything from Imperial.

But Lucy was not about to give up.

Lucy remembered the story in Benjamin Franklin's Autobiography of how he "warmed up" an austere Philadelphian with whom he needed a working *Relationship*. Franklin knew the man had a good private library (unusual, in those days). So Franklin sent him a note requesting the "privilege" of borrowing a rare volume that he knew the man had. Flattered, the man lent the book to Franklin, and this led to the *Relationship* Franklin wanted.

Now Lucy happened to know that Snote is fanatical about gourmet cooking—she even demonstrates the preparation of special gourmet dishes in Global stores.

So Lucy copied Franklin's technique. She wrote a note to Snote respectfully requesting advice on where to buy shallots, truffles and fennel, how to prepare edible ferns, etc. Snote was flattered and gave Lucy the information she had asked for; and later Snote gave Lucy information on the "subgoals" Imperial Products had to meet before Global would consider buying their products. Snote explained the special terms and conditions Global required (credit, deliveries, returns, promotional support, etc.). After Lucy convinced Imperial management to meet these conditions, Lucy came back with the first order Imperial had ever gotten from Global.

Lucy couldn't get to first base when her relationship with Snote was salesperson-buyer. But Snote is a *whole person*, and so is Lucy; and when Lucy reached out to Snote as an expert gourmet, the *Relationship* changed. Only then was Lucy able to learn from Snote the Global "ground rules" that enabled Lucy to make the sale.

Making the Right First Impression

When salesperson and prospect first meet, they begin to evaluate each other. The impressions made on one another tend to be strong and lasting in proportion as they are early. First impressions can be overcome, given the opportunity; but there is also a possibility that this will never happen. It is better to start out on a positive basis and build from there than it is to suffer an unfavorable, negative beginning, and have to try to recover from that, just to get on a "neutral" basis.

The logical strategy for making the right first impression has both negative and positive aspects. Obviously, it calls for avoidance of anything that could be perceived unfavorably by the prospect. But it also calls for the positive manifestation of characteristics which are likely to be perceived favorably—or at least to suggest inclusion within an acceptable category.

The reaction of prospects to their first meetings with salespersons are extremely variable; and can be predicted only to the extent of familiarity with the predisposing and other influential factors in the situation. Some prospects have "built-in" prejudices which affect their reactions to salespeople. These can be directed for or against any evident characteristics, or even characteristics that may only be assumed to exist, on the basis of past associative experience or categorization in disregard of individuality.

Prejudgment is also common and, to some extent, inevitable. A prospect who has never seen a salesperson before will nevertheless have some kind of preconceived perception of him or her even before the initial glimpse. This may be based on such more-or-less indicative considerations as the way in which the prospect views the salesperson's employer; the nature of the products or services to be offered; the way the preliminaries (leading to the call or appointment) were handled; the sound of a voice on the telephone; the appearance of a calling card; the manner in which a receptionist (or other intermediary) announces the caller; etc.

A prospect who does not deal regularly with salespeople will react differently from one whose function it is to deal with many salespeople. Individual prospects range from those who are professionally objective in their dealing, considering only or primarily the competence of the salesperson to function usefully, to those who react with great subjectivity, in terms of whether or not they "like" *this* salesperson.

Conventional wisdom dictates that a salesperson making a first call on a prospect should avoid anything that could reasonably be expected to provoke a negative reaction. Conservative dress, neatness, cleanliness, and strict promptness in keeping appointments are strongly advisable. It is best to avoid aggressive attitudes, undue familiarity, dubious language, eccentricities of appearance or behavior, and any other questionable conduct.

You are there face-to-face with the prospect (presumably on your initiative, but on the prospect's territory); and you are there for a purpose. Since you are there on your own initiative, you are obviously acting in accordance with a purpose that is yours. You need to adapt your purpose to the interests of the prospect, so that the prospect will perceive you as contributing to the fulfillment of some purpose of his or her own. This can only happen if the prospect understands how what you are offering can meet a need or a want that is worth meeting. It may be of equal or greater importance that the prospect "size you up" as at least potentially worthy of being dealt with further. If there is a competitive situation, the prospect must be led to regard you as potentially competitive.

If you represent a well-known company, or one that is known to the prospect, this association may take care of some of the requirements for a first impression that gives you a chance to go on from there. If you are representing only yourself or an organization unknown to the prospect, it may be necessary to "establish your credentials" before your selling will be considered seriously.

All of the above suggestions can be summed up in two rules:

1. Tell who you are, and present what you want to offer in a clear, businesslike way. Be informative so that the prospect gets the impression that you know what you are talking about and are not likely to waste his or her time. This should be the foundation for building an appropriate *Relationship.*

2. Present what you have to offer—as nearly as possible—*in terms of its value to the prospect.* Do this to help the prospect understand why it is to his or her advantage at least to learn more about what you are offering; and to give the prospect a chance to react by asking questions, making objections or presenting facts (so that you can gain insights that will help you to *Communicate* more effectively in Selling the *Benefits).*

If the prospect is a professional, constantly dealing with salespersons, your first approach should emphasize (1) above, and can probably go short on (2). If the prospect is less accustomed to dealing with salespersons—and especially if the prospect is likely to have little familiarity with the kinds of product or service you are offering—then it will probably pay to develop the (2) element.

Since the *Relationship* between salesperson and prospect plays a very important part in most selling; and since the first impression the salesperson makes upon the prospect is almost certain to affect the immediate and subsequent *Relationship*—it is clear that Motivational *Selling* Leverage calls for the salesperson to give serious thought to making the best possible first impression on each prospect.

How Your Opening Can Get
the Prospect to Help You Sell

Your opening with a prospect is an important part of the first impression you make. You may have a "standard opening" ("I'm Pete Marden from Sincere Products, and I'd like to tell you about our new line of neoplastic gismos"). Or you may adapt it somewhat ("Have you seen Sincere's new line of neoplastic gismos? They're the right answer if you have a predilation problem. I'm Pete Marden and I'd like to tell you how they could help"). Or you may have a new opening for a special situation ("You're expanding your predilation departments, so you'll want to know about Sincere's new line of neoplastic gismos. I'm Pete Marden and I'm here to give you all the information your process engineers will need to specify the right installation").

Let's do it again.

Your standard opening: "I'm Nancy George of Loyal Novelties, and I want to show you our new line of Heart-Throb Dainties." Or an adaptation: "There's a new line of Heart-Throb Dainties just out from Loyal Novelties. I'm Nancy George and I'm here to show them to you." Or a new one for a special situation: "I have something here that's just right for your new mid-town boutique. These are absolutely new. They're Heart-Throb Dainties from Loyal Novelties. Here's my card—I'm Nancy George."

Now suppose you are talking to a purchasing agent or a buyer. How much of you does he or she "see" with any of these openings? What would you like him or her to see?

First of all, they see a salesperson.

Purchasing agents and buyers, of course, see salespeople all the time. You know they have heard just about every possible opening; that they usually have their own rather definite ideas about what will and what will not interest them; and that they react to all openings, including yours, in accordance with these ideas.

Basically, they want to know if what you want to sell fits into the pattern of what they need or want. If they need or want what you are selling, you have no problem. If the purchasing agent or the buyer wants it, you don't have to be much of a salesperson. But suppose they don't know of a need. Suppose nobody in their organization has indicated that they want anything like what you have to sell. Then you have a chance to find out what kind of a salesperson you really are.

They may tell you they have no interest in what you offer—and it may seem like a dead end. But if they ever really were a prospect, then there has to be some way to make a sale. There is always that possibility—that chance to break through to a sale. Somewhere in that professional protective armor that so many purchasing agents and buyers seem to wear—somewhere in that plain-spoken lack of interest—there is an opening, and it is up to you to find it.

The best way to discover that possibility is to get them to tell you what it is. And for them to be motivated to do that, they have to "see" you as more than just another uninteresting salesperson.

That means they have to "see" more of you than you showed them in your opening. Basically, they have to "see" you are someone who can help them do their job better, as someone who can tell them something they ought to know.

You want that purchasing agent, or that buyer—or any prospect—to "see" you as a *Whole Person*—and as one who can provide something that will be of benefit to them.

But your opening is something like a move in a chess game—you have to look at least a few moves ahead, or you will be making the wrong move.

Example: The Same Move

SALESPERSON: I'm Pete Marden from Sincere Products. I'd like to tell you about our new line of neoplastic gismos.

PROSPECT A: Aha! Your new line of neoplastic gismos. Good! I've been waiting to hear about them.

PROSPECT B: Yes, I know about the new Sincere line. Have you sold any yet?

PROSPECT C: We're not in the market yet for any kind of gismos.

PROSPECT D: I heard that Apollo Pre-Processing tried out your new line and switched back to paleoplastic gismos.

PROSPECT E: I've already read your literature. Tell me, what kind of a quote can you give me on half a carload, June delivery?

PROSPECT F: After we exhaust our present stock, we won't be using gismos at all.

PROSPECT G: We've been having quality problems with gismos. What is Sincere doing about that?

PROSPECT H: Our people think all gismos are alike. As far as we're concerned, price is the controlling factor. How are you pricing your new line?

PROSPECT I: Our engineers tell me that attaching gismos is the highest cost in our assembly operation. Is your line designed to facilitate assembly?

PROSPECT J: The biggest problem we have, under our product warranty policy, is failure of purchased gismos. Are you guaranteeing the life of your new line?

PROSPECT K: How do they compare with Peabody's new line?

PROSPECT L: How about reliability of supply? We keep our inventories down. We require suppliers to make delivery every Friday afternoon—and bill us as of Monday.

If you look carefully at these examples of possible prospect reactions to Pete Marden's opening (and there are, of course, many other possible reactions), you will note that Pete's opening was "right" only for Prospect A.

But you will also see that each of the other prospects told Pete something, in their reactions, that could help him to learn about their particular needs. Now it is up to Pete. If he can come back with the right *Benefit*, *Communicated* in the right way, he may be on the way to a sale.

But suppose Pete knew, or had taken the trouble to learn, enough about each prospect to use a different opening, appropriately adapted to each specific situation. Wouldn't he make a better, stronger, more effective and productive first impression if his openings, instead of his come-backs, were more like these?

Example:

PETE, TO B: You'll be interested to know that General Molecules is now using our new line of neoplastic gismos in four plants.

TO C: I know your design department hasn't made a decision about gismos yet; but before they do, they should have up-to-date information about our new line.

TO D: Do you know why Apollo Pre-Processing switched back to paleoplastic gismos? It was because they merged with Grenoble; and that's the only kind Grenoble makes. Look at the opening *that* gives *your* marketing people!

TO E: I'm prepared to quote a very attractive introductory price on your immediate requirements.

TO F: We've heard you're switching from gismos to whatsises. But before you do, you ought to know about the improvements in our new line, and how they test against the best whatsises on the market.

TO G: We've designed our new line to meet every complaint we've ever had—especially with new threading on the Pokus. Our Zero Defects Program is the best in the industry.

TO H: Our new line may not be the lowest in price, but I can show you how it will give you the lowest overall costs, when you take assembly and warranty into account.

TO I: Wait till your engineering department sees these diagrams! Our new line attaches in half the time, with no special tools or skill.

TO J: We are so confident of the reliability of our new line that we offer the strongest guarantee in the industry on it.

TO K: We've designed our new line for superiority over all the competition, including Peabody's latest. And we price competitively.

TO L: Our Winchester plant is near enough to yours so we can easily meet just about any delivery schedule with our own trucks.

With openings like these, the prospects' first impression of Pete Marden would surely be that Pete is fully aware of what interests them, and is alert and eager to meet their needs and wants. That is the soundest possible foundation for a productive selling *Relationship*.

Developing a Productive Selling Relationship

Let us consider the essential nature of a *productive selling Relationship*. Fundamentally, the term applies to a *Relationship* between salesperson and prospect or customer that is productive of sales. This principle applies to a one-time sale, as well as to a continuing selling *Relationship*. Obviously, the more frequent and the longer the contacts, the more opportunity there is to develop the *Relationship*.

Any relationship is conditioned by the personalities and values of the people involved and by the circumstances affecting them. Therefore, the relationships a salesperson can develop with prospects ranges from a shared intimacy, with growing common interests, to rigidly formal exchanges, limited to minimum operational procedures. At one extreme, a considerable amount of the whole salesperson will be involved; at the other extreme, the salesperson will bring into the situation only a minimum of himself.

The factors that account for such extremes can best be explained in terms of *role*, which is the term social scientists use in discussing the way people perceive themselves and others.

A woman, for example, plays different roles in her relations with her husband, children, boss, fellow workers, friends, etc. Similarly, a man plays roles that differ according to the way he perceives his relationships with others.

A salesperson calling on a prospect is consciously playing the role of a salesperson and is perceived as a salesperson by the prospect. However, in many situations the salesperson can expand that basic role, bringing more of the Whole Salesperson into the *Relationship* and meeting more of the Whole Prospect.

This process can often proceed to a point where both prospect and salesperson transcend those roles, and appear freed of those role limitations as they engage in social and other non-business activities. This kind of *Relationship* (with the Fulcrum moved quite close to the Weight) enhances the likelihood that the salesperson will receive the information he needs in order to focus on the right *Benefits* and to *Communicate* them effectively, thus gaining maximum Motivation Selling Leverage.

Other circumstances may make it too difficult for the salesperson to expand that role: the prospect may be too cold, too insecure, too busy, too otherwise involved, too influenced by imagined barriers of difference, too inhibited by other obligations, etc. As a result, the salesperson may feel intimidated and uncertain, may not know how to proceed, and may be unable to find (or make) an opening.

In such situations, the relationship will be limited but can still be productive of sales. The salesperson—satisfies the prospect by acting in an approved—or at least acceptable—manner.

In situations like that, the Fulcrum is as close to the Weight as the prospect will allow (and probably as close as it is for any competing salesperson). The *Benefits* involved must be adequately understood on both sides; and the *Communication* about them must meet the requirements of the situation.

If such conditions continue to be met, even that kind of *Relationship* will develop, as the prospect/customer grows used to (and even—to some extent—begins to depend upon) the established selling *Relationship*. The key value here is suggested by such terms as reliability, predictability and dependability.

Example:

Lucy Plitt is a sales engineer for the Admiral Electric Co.; she sells motors and electrical components to manufacturers of electrical products.

Amos Tyndal is the vice president-purchasing of Garside Manufacturing and handles relations with several of his company's suppliers, including Admiral. For years he dealt with Admiral's Butch Gratwick, but Butch has retired and Lucy Plitt has his territory now. Amos has never dealt with a female salesperson and he is uncomfortable with her; he has not learned to accept her, and their relationship is stiff and formal.

However, Lucy is competent and confident. She has been fully briefed on Garside and on Amos Tyndal by her predecessor. She has taken her relationship with Tyndal as a challenge and is determined to win his acceptance.

The most effective way to win him over, she has decided, is to break out of the role of a mere order-taker—the role to which he has confined her—and, instead, become a source of valuable information. Accordingly, at each meeting with Tyndal, Lucy presents at least one item of technical information that is of probable interest to him.

Her progress is illustrated by two meetings, six months apart, of the Garside Executive Committee.

April 6th

PRESIDENT: Anything new in purchasing, Amos?

TYNDAL: As a matter of fact, I have a problem. Butch Gratwick has retired and those idiots over at Admiral have sent a girl—a young girl—to take his place. It's a handicap to me. Of course, I have to give her the routine re-orders; but I haven't figured out yet what to do about our requirements for the products we have under development. Have to find somebody we can work with like I did with Butch. Probably have to go with National or Federal, or maybe import. I'll let you know.

CHAIRMAN: That could be serious, Amos. We depend a lot on Admiral.

TYNDAL: What can I do when I have to deal with a girl?

November 8th

PRESIDENT: Development work on our new torque-balancer has now progressed to the point where we are getting ready for initial production. Amos, you have a list of 18 components we've decided to purchase. Where do we stand on those?

TYNDAL: All ready to go, except for one item—the pre-condensing accumulator.

PRESIDENT: But that's the most important component—and the most expensive.

TYNDAL: That's the reason for the delay. But there's a newly developed insulation that can cut the size and the cost, maybe by half. I'm looking into it now. Lucy Plitt says we'll have a sample to test next week.

PRESIDENT: Who's Lucy Plitt?

TYNDAL: She's with Admiral—took over from Butch Gratwick a while ago. She told me about this new insulation even before Admiral decided to use it in some of their new products; that's why I've been holding off on the pre-condensing accumulators.

CHAIRMAN: Isn't she the one you said was a problem, Amos?

TYNDAL: I said that? She's no problem—no problem at all.

Lucy earned a productive selling *Relationship* with Amos Tyndal by proving that she could be useful to him.

Once a productive selling *Relationship* is developed, it is important to maintain it. The principles are the same as those involved in its development; the salesperson should continue to be sensitive to the values of the prospect.

Relationships are not static—they are living, changing processes of thought and behavior, feelings and acts, motivations and impulses, moods, emotions, impressions and all the other aspects of experience and reaction to it that are a part of our consciousness of other people.

It is very important not to take the *Relationship*—once it is satisfactorily established—for granted. No one likes to feel that anyone else is taking advantage of a *Relationship*. If that happens, the prospect may suddenly become resentful that the salesperson role is so dominant and will revert to the more limited prospect role. That spoils the more expanded *Relationship*—no matter how carefully built up.

Helpfulness and usefulness are practical ways of demonstrating your recognition of, interest in and willingness to further the values that are important to the prospect. Once you establish a pattern of behavior along these lines, and the prospect recognizes this by entering into a warmer, closer, more productive *Relationship* with you, you have committed yourself to continuing that pattern. For if you change—if you "rest on your oars"—you cease to earn that *Relationship*.

Relationships are not like medals, diplomas, or other awards that you win and then get to keep—no matter what. *Relationships* with prospects and customers share, in principle, the same need for continuing contribution as the *Relationship* between husband and wife, parents and child, friend and friend: you have to work at it—or it will go sour.

If you feel that you are putting a lot of extra time and effort (and even tolerance) into building a *Relationship*; and you wonder if it will be worthwhile—remember that there are other rewards you may not have counted on. Believe it or not, there is more to life than making sales. If that is all you think about, you will not only limit your *Relationships*, but you will also limit your sales; and you will be—or become—less of a Whole Person.

Every time you build a mutually satisfying *Relationship*, you change a little (sometimes, a lot); and that makes it easier for you to develop other more satisfying *Relationships*; and helps you to grow, not only as a salesperson, but as a Whole Person. What could be more worthwhile?

★★ 7 ★★
How to Use the Force of Communication: Transaction vs. Conversation

A mechanical lever can be tremendously effective, but it serves no purpose until useful force is applied to it. Similarly, the effectiveness of your selling depends on the force of your *Communication properly applied.*

To apply this force effectively, you have to make your *Communication* motivate the prospect in a positive way.

Doing this requires that you adapt what you say to the needs of the prospect, and you can do this only if you understand what those needs are. You can learn about his or her needs, if:

1. the prospect tells you
2. you listen
3. you really understand

What the prospect *Communicates* is called *feedback*, and it is up to you to understand what the feedback *really* means.

Feedback comes in many forms:

Questions.

Questions tell you that the prospect wants to know more, doesn't understand or remember what you said, or needs to be reassured about something. Be sure to satisfy whatever is *behind* the question. If the prospect is not satisfied by your response, he may ask you, someone else, or themselves more questions, which may weaken the positive motivation you are trying to build.

Objections.

Objections may be based on real doubts, or they may simply be indications of a reluctance or hesitation about buying. An objection tells you something about the prospect's values, and you should respond by focusing on those values. Or you can show that the objection, while valid, does not represent a value that is really important to the prospect.

Resistance.

Determine if the prospect's resistance is simply a strategy to make you sell "harder" or if it is based on reasons which are really important to the prospect. Listening carefully to the prospect and evaluating the feedback should help you to direct your *Communication* so that it will have the greatest effect.

Information.

Some prospects will tell you their needs and may even discuss the values behind them. Such information may come in a neutral way, offered to all potential suppliers, or it may come to you as the result of the special selling *Relationship* you have built with the prospect. When you receive such information, be sure your *Communication* reflects what you have learned and shows that you understand and are reacting constructively to it.

When it comes to making the most of the feedback you get, remember that even the most valuable feedback is worthless to you unless you listen. Listening is really a skill. Listening requires you to concentrate on what the prospect is saying and *not* on what you are going to say as soon as you get an opening.

Many glib salespeople who think they are good communicators are not comfortable unless they are doing the talking; for this reason, what they say is likely to be off the target.

Many of the most successful salespersons listen very carefully and then think before answering. This usually makes a very favorable impression. It indicates to the prospect that what he or she is saying is having an effect. It encourages more feedback and it improves the *Relationship*.

In every selling situation, two fundamental things are happening at the same time. They are so closely related that most people confuse them. Unfortunately, most people (including the salesperson) often do not see or understand the difference, or make the distinction. But the distinction is there, and basic; the salesperson who understands this has a great advantage to begin with.

The salesperson and the prospect are actually involved in *two* simultaneous processes. These are, of course, closely connected, but they *are* different.

One is a *conversation*—an interchange of words—what you *hope* is "the sell." THIS IS *TALK!*

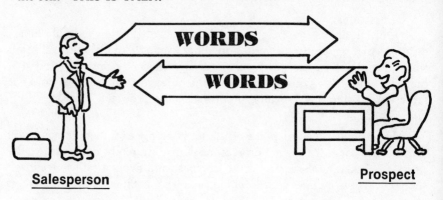

Salesperson   **Prospect**

The other is a *transaction*—an exchange of product or service for money. THIS IS A *DEAL!*

Salesperson   **Prospect**

The talk—the conversation—is the *Communication* you are using as your Force; but not all conversation, of course, helps to make the deal (the sale). Some of the conversation may delay or "kill" the deal. Be sure your *Communication* contributes to the Force you need to "move the prospect." (Sometimes, in building or maintaining your *Relationship* with a prospect/customer, you may indulge in conversation that is not directly related to the deal. But if it helps to build the right selling *Relationship*, it counts as contributing to the transaction.)

If you don't believe these two processes are different, think about it a minute. Remember the times when a customer entered into a transaction with one of your competitors. He bought a similar (or even inferior) product for the same (or even a higher) price. Why?

He could have made the same or a better transaction with you, but he didn't. Why?

Very often, the reason is in the "conversation"—the "sell" didn't make the transaction look good enough. You and he saw the deal differently, and you didn't make him see it your way.

Professional buyers and others who make a career of purchasing, or who are buying for business purposes, usually try to focus on the transaction. They try to concentrate on the "deal"—getting what they need or want at the best value. Sometimes prospects want to eliminate practically all the conversation, or else they almost ignore its effects. But this is rare—and it is even more rare if the salesperson knows how to handle the situation. Even if the prospect wants only to talk price, there *are* other factors.

With other prospects, the conversation usually plays a greater part; sometimes it even outweighs the transaction. When this happens, either the prospect wants only to talk or he has already made up his mind to buy. Conversation will dominate in a selling situation if you have an attractive personality or "just happen to hit it off right" with a prospect. But when you are a *pro*, this can happen quite regularly.

To *make* it happen, you must understand what kind of transaction can be concluded with the prospect and what factors can make it attractive to the prospect. To do this, you must learn quite a bit about your customer, which can be done through skillful control of the conversation. So, when you have utilized the conversation to learn what deal is possible and led your customer to accept it, then you continue using what you have learned to make the sale.

If you have been selling, and have thought about selling, you must have thought something along these lines. But you must also know how it is that, so often, sales are made or lost on what seem trivial considerations—nothing really important; with no significant values apparently involved. Sometimes you don't know or can't understand why a sale was lost. A fuller understanding of the underlying processes can help put more of those "trivial considerations" (which may not really be so trivial) on your side, and fewer on the "no" side. This can greatly improve the odds in your favor. A little improvement here and there can make a lot of difference in the score. The difference between the golf pro's swing and some amateur's swing may not be all that different—but the results are a lot different.

Achieving Positive Motivation by Matching Values

There will be no sale without positive motivation, and the prospect will have positive motivation to buy only if he or she has a good reason to buy. But to make the sale, it is not enough for the prospect to want the benefits you offer; there also has to be a match between the values to the prospect of the benefits you offer and the values to the prospect of the needs that can motivate the prospect to buy. Any values that the prospect perceives in what you are trying to sell will help to motivate the sale, but these values *must be perceived by the prospect.* The mere fact that they are there—or that you believe or know them to be there, or that you believe they *should* satisfy the prospect—has nothing to do with it.

This basic truth may seem simple and obvious but it is so important— and so generally ignored or forgotten by otherwise intelligent sales-persons—that we should go into this point in detail.

What must be done is to get the prospect to realize that there is enough of a *Relationship* between values in what you are offering and values that are within the prospect's own value system. Those are the only values that can motivate the prospect. You may be able to change the prospect's values to match those in what you are offering (which is sometimes known as "educating the prospect" and is discussed later in this chapter). But it is usually necessary to focus on the values that are behind the prospect's needs or wants and show that the values in the benefits you offer can satisfy those needs.

Example: The Easy Prospect

A man enters a drugstore and approaches the prescription counter.

PHARMACIST: Can I help you?

CUSTOMER: I sure hope so! I was entertaining a customer last night and we really overdid it. I have a terrific hang-over—headache, upset stomach, nausea—the whole thing. What do you have that will keep me going? I have important calls to make.

PHARMACIST: Well, I think you should use this.

CUSTOMER: Does it contain aspirin? That sometimes upsets me.

PHARMACIST: OK, take this instead.

CUSTOMER: Anything in it that's bad for a person with high blood pressure?

PHARMACIST: Oh! Then this would be better for you.

CUSTOMER: No sodium, I hope.

PHARMACIST: No, not in this one.

CUSTOMER: Good. How much?

This man was an easy prospect. He needed relief from his discomforts. He identified himself as a prospect for products that could provide certain benefits, but there were also special values associated with his needs that made some products unacceptable. And the pharmacist had to provide a product to match those special values.

Example: Buying Without Being Sold

Josie Sharp went to Total Jeans, a boutique, and approached a clerk who was placing jeans in racks.

"I want jeans I can wear on my boyfriend's boat and a pair of slacks good enough to wear in a nice restaurant."

"What's your size?" the clerk asked. Josie told her.

"Your size jeans are over there, in that rack. You'll find all kinds. Pick out what you want. You can try them on over there, in one of the dressing rooms. As for quality slacks, you'll probably find your size in the rack near that door. When you've found what you want, take them to one of the cashiers."

Josie thanked her, followed her directions, and found what she wanted. No one had to sell her the jeans and slacks. She already had positive motivation to buy, and Total Jeans was organized to help her find the *Benefits* with values that matched her motivation to buy. When she found the jeans and slacks that she had in mind originally (or maybe something she liked even better) she could make a buying decision aimed at the *Benefits* and values she now perceived.

This example illustrates the basic principle of matching the prospect's needs and values with the benefits of what you want to sell. In operating a store like Total Jeans (and there are many stores that operate in this way, including supermarkets and various retail establishments that depend on customer self-service), a large inventory is kept so that prospects can find something that matches their values.

Example: Selling on Paper

Catalogue houses operate on this principle: you have a need or want, so you look in the catalogue, and if you find the right item in the catalogue, you buy it. The people who prepare the catalogue do the selling, and you find the values you need or want for yourself.

Example: Show and Sell

Some people spot an item in a store window and go right in and buy it. Or they see an ad in a newspaper or magazine for an item they may have wanted for a long time or may have only thought about possibly buying someday, or may never have seen or heard about before but that looks good to them, and they write or telephone for it.

In all such cases, the *Benefits* of the item and their values happen to match in the perception of the prospect and this triggers the positive motivation to buy.

Whatever you are selling, always bear in mind that you want to bring about the best match possible between the prospect's needs and wants and the benefits you can offer. The only way to do that is by selling the values (in the benefits you can offer) that match the values that are important to the prospect.

That is the best way to give the prospect a reason to buy.

The Persuasive Process
of Motivational Selling Leverage

Basically, you make a sale by selling the *Benefits, but:*

1. You can sell the *Benefits* more effectively if you have the right selling *Relationship* with the prospect.

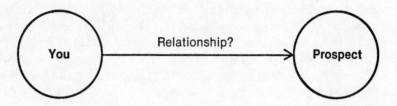

2. You can only sell the *Benefits* by showing that they will satisfy the values involved in the prospect's needs and wants.

| Product Values | ?
 = | Prospect's Needs & Wants |

3. You can sell the *Benefits* and build the right selling *Relationship* by using effective *Communication* (including feedback from the prospect).

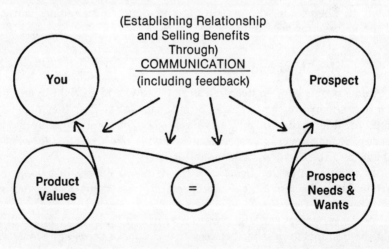

4. When all these factors work together, you can exert effective Motivational Selling Leverage to convert the prospect into a customer.

X

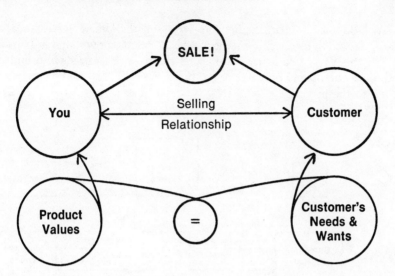

Now, let us look at the way Motivational Selling Leverage functions *as a four-stage process* to bring about motivation to buy.

To begin with, in Stage #1 there are three elements in the situation:

- You.
- The product(s) or service(s) you want to sell.
- The prospect.

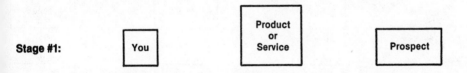

In Stage #2, you sell the benefits to the prospect by *Communicating* how they relate to the prospect's needs or wants.

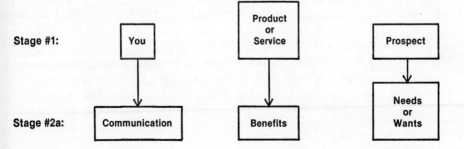

You do this by *selling* the *Benefits*—stressing their values—but you also invite and listen to feedback from the prospect, including questions and objections. In this way, you learn more about the prospect's needs and understand more completely how to present the benefits so they will be more attractive to the prospect.

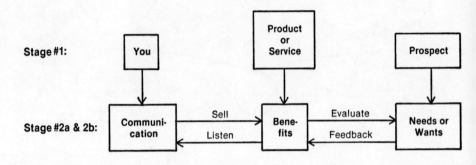

It is at this point that Motivational Selling Leverage is most needed and where it can be most effective to achieve the next stage of the selling process: the matching of values (Stage #3).

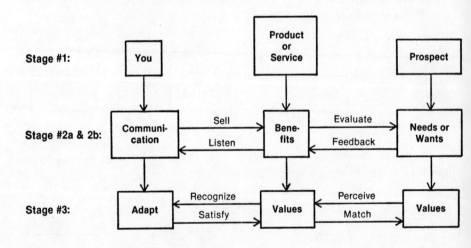

If you do what is needed in Stage #3, the result should be Stage #4: positive motivation to buy—and the buying decision.

These four stages are covered in greater detail in the sections that follow.

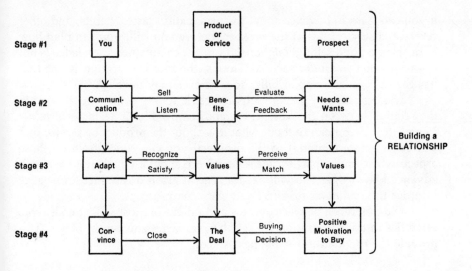

Stage #1: Aiming at the Bullseye

The process of selling begins with three primary elements: the salesperson, the product or service to be sold, and the prospect (Stage #1). The goal of the process, of course, is to bring the three together in a *deal*: a sale of the product or service by the salesperson to the prospect (Stage #4). The selling process involves bringing the three elements into a combination that will satisfy both prospect and salesperson (Stages #2a, #2b, and #3).

In Stage #1 there are many steps that can be taken in advance to improve the selling process. These steps involve the relationship between the salesperson and the product, the relationship between the prospect and the product, and the *Relationship* between the salesperson and the prospect.

All these steps are aimed at making Stage #2 and Stage #3 more effective, and they can be considered as preparatory. In effect, they provide a foundation for the selling of *Benefits* (Stage #2) and the matching of values (Stage #3), and they can make the difference between success or failure.

The steps of Stage #1 that involve the *Relationship* between the salesperson and the product or service are included in what is usually called "product knowledge," which is discussed in the next section.

The steps of Stage #1 that involve the *Relationship* between the prospect and the product or service are also discussed in the next section.

And the steps of Stage #1 which involve the *Relationship* between the salesperson and the prospect are discussed in Chapter 6.

If you can learn in advance about the way the prospect is likely to react to what you are selling, you can adapt your presentation accordingly, and if you can learn in advance about the personality, tastes, habits, and other relevant characteristics of the prospect before you call, you can plan how to develop a good selling *Relationship*. But such advance knowledge is not always available. Under such conditions, the best preparation is one that has the best general applicability to whatever may develop.

The best general preparation applicable to any selling situation is in the relation between the salesperson and the product in terms of *product knowledge*. If you can find out what it is about the product or service that will be of greatest interest to the prospect, you can concentrate on those aspects when you prepare for the selling process; but if you do not have such advance knowledge, you will need a general grasp of product knowledge in order to *Communicate* effectively with the prospect.

The difference between success and failure in most selling endeavors often lies in the preparation. Take whatever steps you can in Stage #1 to provide the foundation for the next stages.

Product Knowledge:
The Key to Selling the Benefits
(Stage #2)

There is no selling tool to match the importance of *product knowledge*. No matter how well you *Communicate*, you cannot be very effective if the prospect concludes that you don't know what you are talking about. (Even the street vendor needs product knowledge to pick the best location, to display his wares effectively, and to make the right "pitch.") Many products and services can only be sold through extensive discussion, during which the offering is hammered out by knowledgeable, experienced individuals on both sides of the deal.

There is no substitute for *product knowledge* and salespeople who have made it their business to gain substantial *product knowledge* will have taken the one most important step toward success in selling.

The ability to *Communicate* may be likened to a gun, which the salesperson aims at a sales target. But a gun is useless without ammunition and *product knowledge* provides that ammunition. The more *product knowledge* you have, the better you can sell the *Benefits* and the more effectively you can establish the *Relationship* between the values in the benefits you are selling and the values that can bring the prospect to a positive motivation to buy.

It is useful to think of *product knowledge* as made up of four different but related categories of information about the product or service to be sold. These are:

A. The nature and characteristics of the product or service itself, including non-obvious potentials, available modifications or extras, etc.

B. Information about the market: uses and applications of the product or service; types of customer and their organizations; and economic and other factors affecting the market. (See page 142.)

C. Information about the supply: competitive or substitutable products or services; competing firms; individuals involved in competition; the economics and practices of production and distribution; pricing and factors affecting price. (See page 144.)

D. Factors related to sales: availability, delivery, inventory, terms, credit, warranty, guarantee or return conditions; maintenance, repair or other services available, etc. (See page 146.)

In many situations, a customer will know more about a product or service than the salesperson who sells it, particularly special uses or applications of what is being sold. The salesperson can learn a great deal from such customers and use this kind of practical information to identify other prospects that he might not otherwise have thought about. In doing this, the salesperson is using *product knowledge* in Categories A and B to develop new sales.

An alert salesperson keeps track of the competition, often using prospect-customer contacts to develop product knowledge in Category C. This is important in order to continue selling to existing customers; it may also produce ideas for selling to prospects more effectively and even to identify new prospects.

When a prospect resists on the basis of price, the sales arguments that can overcome such objections may be found in Category A (emphasizing special features of the product or service that are of particular value to the prospect) or in Category B (pointing out conditions in the market that outweigh the objections) or in Category C (using information about supply, competition, or factors affecting price) or in Category D (when conditions and terms have a special value to the prospect).

Prospects prefer to deal with a knowledgeable salesperson—one whom they respect as a source of reliable information in matters of importance to them. Often, selling *Relationships* can be substantially advanced by providing prospects with information—particularly in Categories B and C—that enable them to meet their own responsibilities more effectively.

In selling products or services that involve complex or technological considerations, product information in Category A becomes especially important, and some prospects facing competitive vendors prefer to deal with the salesperson who provides the most useful information.

PRODUCT KNOWLEDGE

A

The Product or Service

The nature, characteristics, uses and applications.

B

The Market

Factors and developments affecting demand. Customers, prospects. Potential applications and users; listing of approved products and sources.

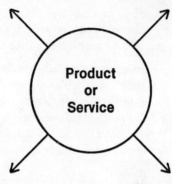

D

Conditions and Terms

Inventories, availabilities, deliveries, terms of payment, credit, discounts, allowances. Modifications, specials, changes and arrangements. Packaging. Service, maintenance, repair, parts availability.

C

The Supply

The competition; possible substitutes. Factors affecting production materials, components, labor, etc. Pricing policies and practices. Economic factors. Developments in redesign, improvement, modification, enhanced functioning; etc.

Example: Skimpy Product Knowledge

Douglas Pindle is an account executive at Fingal and Company, a large brokerage firm. Douglas is new and works mainly on lists of prospects provided by the firm. He relies on information he receives from the firm's Research Department about securities that are recommended as Buy, Hold, or Sell.

Like other account executives, Douglas spends much of his time on the telephone.

DOUGLAS: We are recommending Total Computation. They've had an excellent year; it's selling at 16-3/8, up 1/4 so far today. They're earning $1.95 a share, and we expect them to raise the dividend.

PROSPECT: You think it's a better bet than Super Computation?

DOUGLAS: Well, we don't have that on our Recommended List.

PROSPECT: How many computer companies did you people check out?

DOUGLAS: Let's see, Total is the only one on our Recommended List.

PROSPECT: I'll think about it. Say, anything new on that move by Grimes Consolidated to take over Gresham? Did they raise their bid? I'm holding a lot of Gresham, and I don't know whether to sell now or hold.

DOUGLAS: I'll try to get back to you on that. We don't have a recommendation for Gresham on the list.

Douglas is having a difficult time building up a list of productive customers. His product knowledge is too skimpy to attract investors with experience; they naturally prefer to deal with a broker who provides the information they need.

Rita Diaz is also an account executive with the Fingal firm; she is an "old-timer" who has carefully built up her client list over the years.

Rita's customers have learned to rely on her in making their investments. Here she is on the phone with a customer:

Example: Being on Top of Things

RITA: The market's up a bit since opening because three big banks cut a quarter point off the prime rate. I don't think it'll hold; there's bad news coming out next week on at least four annual reports from major companies. Our research people are recommending Total Computation. They've had a good year, and their latest model is doing well. You can buy it today at 16 and change, but in my opinion it will go lower before it starts to go up because at least five other computer companies will be announcing competitive models in the next couple of weeks. If the whole market sinks, you should be able to pick it up at 15 or maybe even less. Shall I watch it for you?

PROSPECT-CUSTOMER: Thanks, Rita, do that. How about that Gresham you bought me?

RITA: Hang onto it. Colossal is coming into the picture, and they'll be topping the Grimes bid.

PROSPECT-CUSTOMER: Thanks, Rita. I really appreciate the way you keep me informed.

The customer also appreciates the way Rita handles his account. On one occasion he was so impressed with the scope of Rita's knowledge that he asked: "How in the world do you keep up with all those things?" Rita replied: "That's my stock-in-trade. That's what I have to sell. I don't earn commissions by buying and selling. I earn commissions by helping my customers buy and sell on the basis of information that improves their chances of making a profit. If I didn't do that, I wouldn't get any orders."

Product knowledge in the securities business is different from product knowledge in other businesses; but the same principle applies: there is no substitute for *product knowledge* if you want to do a good job of selling.

Using Product Knowledge to Help the Customer

Of all the four categories of *product knowledge,* Categories A and B (knowledge about the product or service and its uses and applications) are the most essential.

Many companies provide extensive training programs for their sales representatives, and they also provide expert back-up in the form of specialists, to help sales personnel to handle difficult customer questions or problems. Many companies employ only salespeople who already possess a high degree of knowledge and experience in the field.

Example: Selling Technology

Teresa Brentano is a chemical engineer by training; she is also a sales representative for Purity Filteraids, Inc., which produces a material (diatomaceous earth) widely used in processing fluids. Teresa's customers include manufacturers of antibiotics, yeast, gelatin, solvents, sugar, and beer.

Teresa usually deals with the highest level of manufacturing executive, with the full acceptance and approval of purchasing agents, who simply receive requisitions and process the orders. Her expertise in the field is highly valued, and she is often consulted by her customers on processing problems. Her customers appreciate the technical help that she provides.

Teresa is not given a fee for this technical help, but she knows that her sales are largely due to such services. Her employers know that, too, and give it recognition in the bonuses they add to her salary.

This kind of selling is increasingly common. Many salespeople have technical backgrounds that they bring to their selling, thus providing their customers with a high degree of specialized knowledge. Such selling is likely to be important when the buying decisions are under the control of technical personnel. In many cases, the salesperson has to deal with a technically oriented purchasing executive—depending on the importance and volume of such procurement.

The knowledge and experience accumulated by a technically qualified salesperson, in the course of helping a series of prospect-customers to solve problems in the uses and applications of products or services, can be of increasing value in developing, serving, and selling an increasing number and variety of prospects.

Example: Product Knowledge Gained the Hard Way

Mark Pulaski sells fine packaging to manufacturers of cosmetics, which requires a highly specialized understanding of multi-color printing processes and the other technical aspects of his field. Mark went to work at Slocum Packaging after graduating from high school and worked his way up from unskilled helper to master printer. Along the way he learned die-cutting, ink-matching, as well as production, layout, and planning.

However, Mark realizes that his "hard-knocks" education is lacking in several essentials, and he is taking college courses at night.

Mark had few advantages to start with and had to work hard to achieve his present level of expertise, and he realizes the importance of learning more. The principle Mark is following is a sound one for all salespeople: the more you know about a product or service, the better you can sell it.

Example: Putting Product Knowledge to Use

Josh Hopkins sells farm equipment for Haskins and Montoya, a dealership in a county that is largely agricultural. Josh was raised on a farm, and he knows about tractors, combines, harrows, and planters.

He is watching TV with his wife on a spring evening when the telephone rings. It is Jeremy Cluger, a dairy farmer who operates a herd of 200 Holsteins. Jeremy bought a complete installation of milking equipment from Josh two months ago.

"I started milking at four o'clock, eight at a time, like always; then about five o'clock the dang machines stopped working. I've got close to a hundred cows yet to be milked and they're bellowing their heads off. There's no way I can milk that many by hand, and I can't get the dang machines going again!"

Josh is in the Cluger "milking parlor" in twenty minutes and goes over the installation hastily but with expert thoroughness. He soon finds the trouble—a stuck valve in the vacuum system—and fixes it. Then he pitches in to help Jeremy make up for lost time.

Jeremy and a lot of other farmers in the area would never think of buying equipment from anyone but Josh. They recognize not only his extensive *product knowledge* but also his complete dedication to applying it for their benefit. They know they are not only buying the equipment, but also the continuing interest and great helpfulness—backed by *product knowledge*—that they can count on from Josh Hopkins.

That makes all the difference in their buying decisions. There is no substitute for using *product knowledge* to help the customer.

How Knowing the Market (Demand) Helps You Sell (Category B)

Consider carefully each of the following propositions about the market in which you are selling.

1. If you have an absolute monopoly in your market, you will need to know a lot about it if you are to do the best that you can with it. Many good products and services that were original and unique never got off the ground because of poor marketing.

2. If you are selling in a highly competitive situation, you cannot do well without knowledge and understanding of the market. You have to: find prospects who will prefer to do business with you; know what segments of the potential market are most promising for you; be aware of developments and trends of which you can take advantage; and know how to take advantage of them. In competitive markets, the business often goes not to the "best" product or service or even to the lowest priced offerings but to the most knowledgeable salesperson.

3. Your prospect usually knows a lot about the market, and you will be at a disadvantage if you do not know even more. Many prospects do a lot of shopping around before they buy; they also read advertisements, send for sales literature (catalogues, brochures, etc.), and even telephone or visit to check on user evaluations. And, of course, they talk to other salespeople.

When you deal with prospects who have some knowledge of the market, you will want to take advantage of anything favorable to you—and to counter anything unfavorable—that they may have heard or read; and the more you know about the market, the better you can do it. In fact, if the prospects know—or think they know—something you don't, their respect for and confidence in you will suffer, and that kills the *Relationship* you need for Motivational Selling Leverage. So, to sell a prospect who has alternative sources in the market, you will need to know more than he or she does.

4. Knowledge about the market includes the uses and applications of the product or service. Such knowledge provides a basis for understanding the needs and wants of prospects and for matching *Benefits* to their values.

Category B of *product knowledge* includes all matters related to the demand aspects of the product or service: knowledge about or related to the prospects and customers, and potential prospects and customers, for the product or service. The information in Category B concerns the demand aspects of the information you will need about the marketplace. (The complement to this involves the supply aspects, Category C of product knowledge, which is discussed on page 144.)

Whether you are calling on a great many prospects or customers, or are putting in full time on only one customer, you still need all the market information that may be relevant to your prospect's/customer's interests.

Example: Not Knowing the Market

The Gross Chemical Company distributes its products through salespeople who are assigned territories and who sell on commission. The president of the company has employed a marketing consultant to increase sales volume. The consultant, John Murray, is presenting an oral report.

"Your top sales producer in Ohio got 87 percent of his volume from 11 products, and there were 43 of your products he never sold. Your top sales producer in Pennsylvania got 76 percent of her sales from 14 products, and only three of these products were among the 11 that did well in Ohio. The best sales producer you have is in New Jersey, and she doesn't have one garage, bakery, restaurant, hotel or motel on her list of customers—all her volume is in sales to chemical and pharmaceutical plants. I told her you could put three other salespersons in the same territory; tell them to stay out of chemical and pharmaceutical plants, and they'd still do very well with all the other prospects she doesn't sell, without taking a nickel from her.

"The simple fact is your salespeople do not know their market. They learn how to sell one kind of prospect, and they stick with that. For instance, you have about 7 products that can be sold to machine repair shops, transmission specialists, and automobile and truck servicing operations. Your people in western Massachusetts, Oregon, and South Carolina get almost all of their volume from such sales but ignore the rest of the market. On the other hand, your people in Idaho, Mississippi, and New Hampshire get practically all of their volume from the food business—restaurants, food processors, etc.—and just about never call on machine shops or auto repair operations.

"I estimate that even the best of your salespeople are contacting only about 16 percent of their potential market."

The condition that John Murray spotted is common and is the despair of many sales managers and marketing executives. Many salespeople lose out on sales because they don't realize how many prospects there actually are. Sometimes they feel confident or comfortable with only one kind of prospect with whom they have had some success and therefore feel that they only know how to sell to other prospects in the same line. But in restricting themselves, they are surrendering a great earning potential.

This is particularly true when the salesperson is representing a line of products with diverse uses and applications. A salesperson carrying such a line does not know which items can meet the prospect's needs. Leaving a catalogue, brochure, or a list of products for the prospect to pick and choose from is no substitute for knowing which items to offer and then selling the *Benefits* that have value for the prospect.

Having a number of products to offer constitutes a broadening of the opportunity to sell. That opportunity is denied to the salesperson who sells one kind of product or service to only one kind of prospect.

Learn all you can about the *demand* side of your market: *Who* are the obvious prospects? Who are the *potential* prospects? And think about how to make these prospects your customers. Only in this way can you develop the sales volume that can be developed from the demand potential in the market you serve.

Knowing the Supply Side of the Market (Category C)

The supply side of the market involves three selling principles, which are detailed in this section.

A. What you and/or your company are doing, can do and are planning on doing for present and potential prospects/customers.

Many salespeople attempt to sell without knowing all the products or services they could offer. It is important to be fully informed about what your company can provide.

Example: Not Knowing Your Company's Capabilities

ARTHUR B (SALESPERSON): I thought they were going to buy a thousand or more of our Model 16B; but they wanted it with controls on the left side and a three-pole switch.

MARY F (SALES MANAGER): Call them up right away and tell them we can provide those at the same price, if they'll order at least 800. We do make modifications like

> that when the quantities justify it. I
> thought you knew that! I'd hate to
> lose a sale like that just because you
> didn't know we could deliver!
>
> ARTHUR B: So would I!

Many sales can be made by adapting a product or service to meet a prospect's demand. This often calls for adjustments in price, delivery, quantity requirements, fulfillment during slack times, etc. The salesperson who knows how to sell such "specials" can develop sales others would miss. And working with a prospect or customer on such sales is one of the best ways to develop a selling *Relationship* that will lead to other sales.

B. Know what your competition can do for present customers and potential prospects.

If you try to sell to a prospect who knows what your competition is offering while you do not, you will probably be at a great disadvantage in selling advantageously the *Benefits* of the product or service you offer. You should be selling the *Benefits competitively*—demonstrating that what you offer will meet the needs of the prospect better than the competition. But you can't do that if you don't know enough about the competition.

You need to direct your selling at how the prospect perceives the offerings of the competition in relation to his or her needs; otherwise the prospect will be influenced by considerations you know nothing about.

In addition, the competition may be introducing new or improved products, or new price structures, terms, warranties, etc. Many companies rely on their sales force to uncover such vital information about competitors, and they want it soon enough to do something about the situation.

Sometimes a prospect will delay a planned purchase while awaiting the introduction of new or improved products, price reductions, etc. The salesperson who has to sell against such an obstacle should be aware of such expectations.

C. Know the developments that may affect supply by introducing improvements, substitutes, changes in material, design, function, price, etc.

Everything changes; products and services are created, developed, and disappear along with their markets. Some new products and services bring entirely new markets into being, while others simply replace older products and services. In our dynamic economy, the market for any product or service may be seriously affected by some development in a totally different field. You don't have to think in terms of automobiles replacing horses; there are similar but less dramatic changes taking place around us all the time in every market. Such changes affect the selling of existing products and services and offer challenging opportunities to salespeople who are alert enough to grasp them.

Example: Finding Sales Opportunities

Marshall Jellinek sells yard goods for a textile company that specializes in synthetic fabrics. He has made an appointment to see his sales manager, Dom Mongello.

> DOM: Hi, Marsh, what's on your mind?
>
> MARSHALL: I need to know something from Production—and the sooner the better.
>
> DOM: OK! Let's have it!
>
> MARSHALL: How long would it take to produce 100,000 yards of a special strength synthetic—say about twice as heavy as our Number 3187, and what would it cost?
>
> DOM: We don't make anything like that now. We could, I guess, but who wants it?
>
> MARSHALL: Brogwynne Contracting.
>
> DOM: They're a small customer and very seasonal.
>
> MARSHALL: They used to be, Dom. They're under new management now, and the new guys have put in bids on government work. I just read that Brogwynne has been awarded an Air Force contract for cargo parachutes—more than $6,000,000 worth. We can sell them the fabric, but I need to know a lot of details from Production. You know I have to make sense on my first call about this deal; if I do, they'll tell me whatever we need to know in order to make the winning proposal on supplying the cloth for all those chutes.
>
> DOM: You'll get it, Marsh. I'll see to that!

Sales opportunities often come from directions not easily anticipated. But the salesperson who looks for opportunities in an imaginative way and who is able to recognize an opportunity when it occurs—that is the salesperson who will cash in while others envy and wonder why they didn't have "that luck."

It is possible to "make a lot of luck for yourself"—and the way to do it is to go after it, in the right place, where nobody else happens to be looking. That may not be easy, but it can be *very* worthwhile.

How the Conditions of Sale
Affect the Buying Decision (Category D)

To satisfy the needs of the prospect, you may have to offer *Benefits* that are not integral elements of the product or service you are selling. The values that determine the prospect's buying decision are often related to conditions or terms under which the product or service will be provided. If such conditions or terms are important to the prospect, they constitute values which will be decisive in determining who gets the order, and the salesperson who best understands such special values and knows how to accommodate them will be most likely to make the sale.

Example: When a Sale Depends on the Mode of Payment

SALESPERSON: I came by to pick up the order.

BUYER: Sorry; we're giving the order to Elphinstone.

SALESPERSON: But we've met your specifications, and we're offering you as low a price as you'll find in the industry—lower than theirs, I'm sure.

BUYER: That's true, and we'd like to do business with you but we can't.

SALESPERSON: Why not?

BUYER: This is a big order, and it ties up a lot of money. Elphinstone is willing to carry us for six months, until we can turn over our stock. We'll be giving up your discount that depends on payment in 10 days; the Elphinstone deal calls for interest to be paid after 60 days. But their deal will cost us less than buying from you and borrowing from our bank. And we won't be tying up our bank credit limit, either.

SALESPERSON: But our product is as good as Elphinstone or better, and our price is right.

BUYER: That's true. But if you figure the problem and the costs of financing the purchase, we're making a better deal.

Any prospect worth a salesperson's time expects to pay for products or services received, but the arrangements for payment can vary over a very wide range of terms and accommodations. Often, there are common financing practices in a particular line of business, but there are opportunities for "creative financing"—the tailoring of payment to fit the special needs of a prospect.

Example: When a Sale Depends on a Time Factor

Nat Kriendler is a salesman for Humperdink Equipment, a firm that rents or leases heavy equipment to contractors. He is talking to Gus Fortunato, general manager of Lombardi Construction.

GUS: That's an impressive list of machines, and a lot of them are the kinds we use. The prices look about right. I think maybe we can do a little business.

NAT: Great! How soon?

GUS: Well, I'll give you a try right now. I see you have 3 Earthworm Number 8 bulldozers on your list. We're starting a job in Bensonville, and we'll need two like that. How soon can you put them on the site?

NAT: Can I use your phone? (Nat calls his office.)

GUS: (As Nat hangs up the telephone): Well?

NAT: We can give you one by the end of next week and another in about three weeks. They're both out on jobs; the third is on a long-term lease.

GUS: We need them sooner than that. We're working against time and a penalty clause, and we're planning to break ground on Monday. We'd pay you a bonus if you meet our schedule. We're talking about long leases and more business.

NAT: Gus, I'd give anything to close a deal like that with you, but I told you what my boss said—and I can't change that!

(Next day)

NAT'S BOSS: So how'd you make out at Lombardi?

NAT: I was going great with Gus, and he was all set to lease two of our Earthworm 8's, long term—with a bonus—if we could spot them on the site by Monday. But you told me they were all tied up.

NAT'S BOSS: Oh, no! Why didn't you tell me all that? All you did was ask about our current status on the Earthworms. One of them is in the shop for routine overhaul—but we could have done that with overtime and have completed it during the weekend. The other is on a small job in Pound Ridge; we could have gotten them to release it and given them a 6 instead. We could have met Gus's deadline—if only I'd known yesterday morning what you're telling me now.

Often, time is a major factor in a selling situation, and meeting the time requirements is of primary value to the prospect. Other examples include the retailer who is out of stock on a "hot" item and eager to get in a new shipment while the demand is active and the manufacturer in urgent need of equipment or material for processing a new order against a promised delivery date. Unexpected events, such as fires, tornadoes, and other destructive occurrences often generate requirements for immediate delivery of equipment, materials, supplies, replacements, etc. In many situations, price is not nearly as important as timeliness. For prospects who face such situations, the suppliers who can be relied upon to help them meet schedules are valued above others, and the salesperson who is helpful to them will do well indeed.

Example: Selling Other Factors

Maude Ryan sells a line of metal fittings to manufacturers of wooden furniture. She is calling on Dwight Logan, director of purchasing for Whitlock and Page.

MAUDE: I know you like our line and our prices are competitive. We also offer attractive discounts for regular purchases in certain quantities.

DWIGHT: I do like your line and your prices, but we've been dealing with Glen Falls Specialties for years and I see no reason to change.

MAUDE: Do you ever run short and have to have delivery in a hurry?

DWIGHT: Once in a while. When we get a rush order, we may use up our inventory and run short before we can get a new shipment.

MAUDE: Glen Falls is about, what, 800 miles from here? At least a couple of days or more by train or truck?

DWIGHT: If we need it badly enough, they fly it down.

MAUDE: And that costs!

DWIGHT: That's true.

MAUDE: They can only do that *if* they have it in stock! You know where we are? About two miles from here—a half-hour away. And we always keep a full inventory on hand.

DWIGHT: I don't know. . . . I'll talk to our production people; they may think that would make a switch worthwhile.

MAUDE: That isn't all. You have a plant in Canada; so do we, not far from yours. We know you're setting up a plant in Saudi Arabia to assemble furniture from parts you'll ship from here. We do a substantial export business, and we know how to pack and expedite export shipments.

DWIGHT: Well, you've brought up some points that are important to us. Let's see, come back Thursday. I'll talk to production and export, and I may have news for you.

There are many factors beside the product or service itself and the price that can determine the buying decision. And the salesperson who is aware of such factors and knows what to do about them is the one most likely to win the order.

Stages #2 and #3 of the Process:
Shooting at the Bullseye

If you have ever fired any kind of weapon at a target, you know that you cannot hit the bullseye without taking careful aim. You probably have to adjust your aim to allow for distance and for the wind. If the target is moving you have to "lead" it.

Selling is a lot like that, except for one very big difference: when you are selling, you may not even "see" the target, or know what part of the target is the bullseye. You may be able to hold your weapon steady and "squeeze" the trigger with great skill—but none of that will help if you shoot in the wrong direction, at the wrong target, or at the wrong bullseye.

To carry this comparison a little further, knowing *how* to aim and shoot is like knowing *how* to sell; knowing *where* to aim is like knowing *what* to sell. *What* you should be selling may not be easy to know; because it is not just "the benefits," but the particular *Benefits* that fit the values that are important to the prospect. Once you have figured out what those particular *Benefits* are, and just how they relate to the values important to the prospect, *then* it is up to you to *sell* them as effectively as possible.

It is best not to think of the *prospect* as a target. A person is only a prospect when there is a chance he or she may react with positive motivation to the benefits you offer. That means your real target is whatever can cause that positive motivation. Within that target, the bullseye is that particular perception of the *Benefits* you offer, which really fits the needs and wants—the values—of the prospect so well that the positive motivation to buy actually results in a decision to buy.

It is your *Relationship* with the prospect that provides the opportunity to learn what you need to know about the target. Show by appropriate statements, good questions, listening, and careful evaluation of feedback that you are interested, knowledgeable, and able and willing to understand the prospect's very special concerns. The prospect will almost certainly respect this in you, and appreciate it; and you will be building the selling *Relationship* you need, bringing the Fulcrum ever closer to the Weight.

With the knowledge you gain about the target and the bullseye, you can focus on the *Benefits* that are most appropriate. This gives you a longer lever arm, for greater Motivational Selling Leverage. The better you understand the prospect's special and particular values, the more effectively you can present the appropriate *Benefits* in ways that will have greatest appeal. This kind of effective *Communication* gives you the Force that makes the most of your Motivational Selling Leverage.

The comparison with shooting may be made clearer if we think in terms of artillery spotting. The battery fires at the target, using the best available

MOTIVATIONAL SELLING LEVERAGE

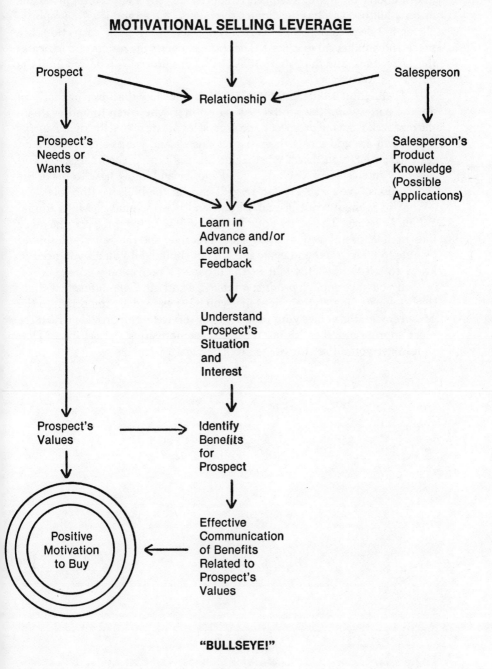

Prospect → Relationship ← Salesperson

Prospect's Needs or Wants

Salesperson's Product Knowledge (Possible Applications)

Learn in Advance and/or Learn via Feedback

Understand Prospect's Situation and Interest

Prospect's Values → Identify Benefits for Prospect

Positive Motivation to Buy ← Effective Communication of Benefits Related to Prospect's Values

"BULLSEYE!"

151

information from maps, intelligence reports, etc. There is a spotter in a plane or on a hilltop, and he coordinates the bursts. "Over and left," he reports. "Bring it 2 degrees right and shorten range 400 yards." The corrections are made and another salvo is fired. The spotter reports the results and indicates the corrections, and the battery fires again. The process is repeated until the battery is "on target."

Well, good selling *Communication* is a lot like that, except that *you* are the battery *and* the spotter. As the spotter, you listen to and evaluate the feedback from the prospect to determine if you are selling the right *Benefits* and if you are addressing the prospect's needs and wants effectively. And (as the spotter) you detect whether or not the prospect is interested—and just how interested. If you are a good spotter and know how to make the "corrections," you will get "on target" and hit the bullseye (the sale).

This is the essence of real selling; and it is the goal of Motivational *Selling* Leverage. The better your *Relationship* with the prospect, the more informative, useful feedback you should receive; and the better you should be able to understand and evaluate it. That should tell you all you need to know to sell the *Benefits* that fit the prospect's needs and wants.

If you have enough *product knowledge* and can *Communicate* it effectively, you can match the values that you have learned are important to the prospect with the values your product(s) or service(s) can provide which are most appropriate to satisfying those values motivating the prospect. That should get you all set for Stage #4 (The Deal).

★★ 8 ★★
Dynamic Selling Leverage Tactics for Closing More and Bigger Sales

Six Conditions Essential to Closing a Sale (After Positive Motivation)

In many selling situations there *are* unfavorable conditions to be met and overcome before a sale can be closed. The salesperson needs to make an analysis of such situations to identify the unfavorable conditions and indicate whether or not they are controllable in any degree.

It is impossible to list all the conditions that may present difficulties in the closing of a sale. But it is possible to present a basis for classification of unfavorable conditions; and this should be helpful to the salesperson in overcoming resistance in many selling situations.

Essential Condition #1:

Knowing that a decision to buy results from positive motivation, let it be clear that the positive motivation to buy, all by itself, is not enough. Positive motivation satisfies the first basic requirement: that the prospect must want or need the products or services offered. That is Essential Condition #1. But there are five other Essential Conditions which must be met before the prospect is ready to buy.

Up to now we have discussed the absolute necessity for positive motivation of the prospect. We have also discussed, as Essential Condition #1 for Making a Sale, the positive motivation arising from the prospect's perception of the value of the *Benefits* to be provided by the product(s) or service(s) offered to satisfy the prospect's needs or wants.

However, positive motivation to buy, based only on Essential Condition #1, may not be enough. The prospect may have substantial positive motivation to buy, based on Essential Condition #1, and still not be ready or willing to make the purchase. If so, that will almost certainly be because one or more of five other Essential Conditions for Making a Sale have not been met.

It is of the utmost importance that the salesperson understand the nature of these five other Essential Conditions for Making a Sale, so that he or she may be alert to the possibility of their not being met, and will know what to do about such a situation.

There is no question that Essential Condition #1 is the most important of the Six Essential Conditions—in fact, it is indispensable. The prospect can have no rational, realistic, ethically acceptable positive motivation to buy* unless there is a recognized need or want for the *Benefits* offered. If this Essential Condition #1 is not met, the other five either cannot apply (#2, #5, #6) or do not matter (#3, #4). If and when Essential Condition #1 is met (or when it is close to being met), then any of the other five Essential Conditions may be of such critical importance as to have the sale depend upon it's being resolved satisfactorily.

In this section we will discuss Essential Conditions #2, #3, #4, #5 and #6 for Making a Sale; in the following sections we will discuss how to overcome the difficulties that may be encountered in meeting and satisfying all six conditions so that you can close the sale successfully.

To begin with, let us identify and outline these five Essential Conditions for Making a Sale that are in addition to Essential Condition #1—the satisfaction of needs or wants.

Essential Condition #2:

The prospect must find the conditions of purchase (including price, terms of payment, delivery, etc.) acceptable. Some aspect of this is almost always a major factor in the decision to buy, and one in which competition often plays a major role. But there are more ways to handle price problems than most salespersons know or use.

The Essential Condition (other than #1) which is most often of critical importance is #2. Many purchases are made on a price comparison basis, often on competitive bids. Behind such buying is the assumption that each would-be vendor—you and your competition—is offering the same or equivalent *Benefits*. This is usually made more or less explicit in the stated specifications, but it may be merely an implicit assumption on the part of the prospect. In either case, if your price is higher it is up to you to show that you are offering *Benefits* that have enough additional value to the prospect to justify it. Similarly, certain other conditions of sale, such as terms

---

*Possible exception: preemptive buying.

of payment, credit, discounts, or delivery, may be of critical importance to the sale. You must be able to discover any such negative conditions if they are not made clear by the prospect, and you must be able to negotiate them satisfactorily.

Essential Condition #3:

The prospect must be willing to make the purchase from the saleperson or with the company that the salesperson represents.

There are a number of problems that may arise in meeting this condition, which are discussed later in this chapter.

Essential Condition #4:

The prospect must feel free to make the purchase.

Such freedom may be affected by many factors—legal, organizational, budgetary, bureaucratic, "political," etc. This condition is also discussed later in this chapter.

Essential Condition #5:

The prospect must believe that the purchase is "a good buy" in terms of the values that are important to the prospect.

This condition is most likely to be met when Conditions #1 and #2 are satisfactory, and it may overcome obstacles to Conditions #3 and #4.

Essential Condition #6:

The prospect must believe that the purchase should be made *now*.

Delays, of course, can kill a sale. The problems of delay and what to do about them are discussed later in this chapter.

Any or all of these six conditions must (usually) be met, if they arise. They may present varying and unpredictable kinds and degrees of difficulty, and the existence and representations of competitors may greatly complicate the situation. Salespersons therefore often ignore one or more of the essential conditions while concentrating elsewhere; this often results in wasting time and effort on one or more conditions that are unimportant or already effectively met, while leaving other essential conditions unsatisfied.

Salespeople sometimes lose sales by concentrating on one or two of these conditions and therefore end up by losing out on one they have ignored.

Example: Forgetting the Competition

Howard Green represents a company that offers a line of training materials for supervisors and "motivational" posters to boost employee concern for safety and productivity. There is a large plant in his territory that he has never been able to "crack," but now they have a new director of personnel and Howard is making another try. The new man listens attentively, shows interest, and accepts samples of Howard's line for study. Howard is suddenly optimistic about this prospect.

When he calls again, a month or so later, he is greatly disappointed. The director of personnel had indeed become interested in Howard's line and inquired of other personnel directors about their experience with such materials. He soon learned that there were similar materials available from other sources and that some of these were regarded as superior to Howard's line. After investigating, he decided to use one of these competitive lines.

Howard had worked to meet Condition #1 but he had not done anything—or enough—about Conditions #2 and #3. He lost the sale through failure to follow up, which could have made him aware of the situation and enabled him to address those conditions.

Example: Forgetting to Sell More Than Product or Price

Dick Talbot is the East Coast representative of a California company that offers a line of ventilating equipment for installation in office buildings, hotels, factories, and other large structures. He is calling on an architect with an important firm in New York City, which has been retained to draw plans for a large residential development near Hartford, Connecticut. In the plans for this housing project, Dick wants the architect to specify the use of some of the products he can offer.

He convinces the architect that his products are equal or superior to those available elsewhere and that the cost is lower than the competition. He leaves, convinced that he will get the order.

But he doesn't. A sharp competitor points out to the architect that equipment of the type involved requires replacement parts from time to time and that a California company could not provide these without a very inconvenient delay. The competitor, with a plant located in Massachusetts, gets the contract.

Too late, Dick realizes that in addition to meeting Conditions #1 and #2, he should also have been meeting Condition #3 by telling the architect about his company's plan to establish a warehouse in New Jersey to stock replacement parts. Dick could have covered this point, which would have determined the buying decision in his favor, but he didn't.

Example: Forgetting to Sell More Than the Company

Allen Booth represents a division of HEXCO Petroleum, one of the largest oil companies in the country. The division manufactures plastic parts under contract, using materials from other divisions of its parent organization. The field is extremely competitive.

Allen is offering to produce a regular supply of specially molded plastic parts for a manufacturer of kitchenware. He is talking to the vice president–manufacturing of the Super-Chef Kitchenware Company. Allen emphasizes that Super-Chef will be dealing with HEXCO Petroleum—using the prestige and size of that huge organization to get the order.

Allen doesn't get the order. While he was concentrating on his assumed advantage in meeting Condition #3, a competitor was doing an excellent job in meeting Condition #2, and certain specialized aspects of Condition #1. And the Super-Chef people weren't overwhelmed by the opportunity to deal with a small part of HEXCO.

Allen didn't realize that the values most important to the Super-Chef people were much more in the areas of Conditions #1, #2, #4, #5 and #6 than they were in Condition #3.

Closing the Sale When a Prospect Thinks Your Price Is Too High

The most common obstacle to a sale is price. This need not prevent the sale if you follow these steps.

A. Evaluate the price problem in detail. Develop answers to such questions as:

1. Does the prospect have *enough* positive motivation to buy?

2. Is the prospect considering a competitive offer? If so, how does it compare in satisfying needs and wants, in matching prospect values, and in price?

3. Consider your own price: how much lower would it have to be to meet the prospect's objections? And can anything be done about that? (Often, a lower price can be arrived at by changes in certain conditions: terms of payment, time and conditions of delivery, warranties or guarantees; also changes in size, grade, model, quality, packaging, container, etc.; modifications of specification; or reduction of unit price by increasing the size of the order.)

B. Review the prospect's values that brought about the positive motivation to buy. What value is behind his or her interest in your product? In your competitor's offering?

1. Can you emphasize or strengthen these in order to justify the price?

2. If competition is a factor, develop convincing comparisons between the benefits you offer and those offered by the competition to justify your higher price.

3. Demonstrate why your offering should be priced higher than the competitive offering.

4. Review carefully the status of the six conditions and determine what can be done to increase their importance to the prospect.

Clearly, the better your *Relationship* with the prospect, the easier it will be to develop the information and the insights indicated under A and B and the better opportunity you will have to apply the results toward overcoming price resistance and moving to close the sale.

Example: Stressing Extra Values

Jud Brennigan is a contractor who is bidding on the construction of a home in a high-status suburb; he is talking to the architect, who thinks Jud's bid is high.

"Yes, I see that I'm about $3000 higher than Munat. But let's look at the reasons. I'm putting in all copper tubing; Munat is using plastic. On this house, that'll make a difference of about $800 for the cheaper materials and maybe $600 for less labor. For a house of this quality, you should be using copper, and I feel your client would agree. It's ratproof and it won't mold; it's there for as long as the house. If you insist on plastic, I can put it in and knock off $1200 to $1500, but I'd hate to do it.

"Then there's the air conditioning. I'm putting in at least 40 feet more duct work than Munat—and you need it. And I'm putting in a bigger septic tank and twice as big a field of tile. Why? Because the soil is heavy and rocky.

"You're designing a high-class house, and I'm trying to build it for you. We're talking $3000 on a $300,000 bid—about 1 percent more to do things right. Do you want that or do you want me to compromise like Munat?"

Jud won that argument. The architect agreed with him and sold his clients on the values ("quality") they would be getting for the extra $3000.

Example: Justifying a Bigger Price

Benton Swales sells flowers wholesale for a major grower with hothouses and nurseries near a big city. He is talking to Aristotle Antigopoulos, owner of a successful florist shop.

AA: How much are your long-stemmed Elinor roses, Ben?

BS: The way you're buying them now, Ari, they're $17.50 a dozen. And ours are the best in the market—you'll admit that.

AA: They're nice, but they're too high. I sell them for $24 a dozen; and I can buy them for $12 from Dunlap. That gives me a 100 percent markup—which I need—what with the loss from wilting, spoilage, broken stems, and all that.

BS: Just how many do you sell in a week, Ari?

AA: Oh, I average a couple of gross or thereabouts. More, of course, on holidays and in the busy seasons.

BS: Ari, you can sell a lot more of ours than you can of Dunlap's, if you put them in that window and let people see how beautiful they are. And you can buy ours for less if you take enough of them.

AA: Tell me more.

BS: You agree to buy two gross of our higher quality roses every week and three or four gross for Christmas, Mother's Day, Valentine's Day and so forth. If you do that, you get them for $15 a dozen. We'll deliver twice a week—and we'll pick up the spoilage and credit you with half what you paid for it. I know Dunlap doesn't do that. Altogether, that ought to be a helluva good deal for you.

AA: Ben, I think I'll try that for a month and see how it goes.

Ben overcame the price resistance by offering higher quality, promising to pick up half the cost of spoilage, and reducing his original price. He justified the price reduction by substantially increasing the quantity and making the sale a regular, weekly transaction. And he was still selling his Elinor roses for more than the competition.

Example: Tailoring a Sale to a Budget

Rodney Brisk sells a line of maintenance materials to factories, office and apartment buildings, and hotels. He usually deals with someone in charge of maintenance. Rodney has been taking an order for a number of items from Merce Pote, manager of maintenance for a large refinery.

RB: Thanks, Merce; that's a nice order. I know you're in a hurry for it, so I'll get on it right away.

MP: Wait a minute, Rod. Add it up. I've got to know how much I'm spending. I am on a budget, you know.

RB: OK. Let's see. (Adds.) Well, Rod, the total is $5,491.82.

MP: Wow! I didn't realize. That would put me way over my budget for the month.

RB: Well, let's see. Take that Super-Power Vac. That's $920. Do you need that right away? And how about that extra set of power wrenches? They're $720 a set and you ordered two sets.

MP: Right, Rod. Cancel the Super-Power Vac and one set of power wrenches. That's over $1600 off this month's order; so it's OK to go ahead with the rest. And Rod, don't forget to put that Super-Power Vac and that set of power wrenches down for next month.

Overcoming the Obstacle of Being an Unacceptable Source

Prospects often have adverse attitudes toward companies, products, services, trade names, or individuals; and these attitudes can affect their buying decisions. Such "thinking" may be hopelessly illogical, completely outdated, totally ill-founded, or quite irrelevant—but can still influence a buying decision against an otherwise preferable vendor. A prospect may not even be conscious of the effects such notions are having on his or her evaluation of factors affecting the buying decision.

If and when you encounter sales resistance that you cannot satisfactorily account for as resulting from inadequate motivation to buy, or similar negative conditions, you should consider the following possibilities.

1. The prospect may have had an unpleasant experience with another salesperson or another individual with your firm.

2. The prospect may have had an unsatisfactory experience with a product or service provided by your firm.

3. The prospect may have had an unfavorable reaction to something he has read or heard about your firm.

4. The prospect may have had some resented experience with your firm, other than as an actual or potential customer.

5. The prospect may have an adverse reaction to you personally.

6. The prospect may simply be reflecting his or her organization's reaction to an unfavorable report—which may not be accurate—about your firm, the product or service you are offering, or yourself.

The best course to pursue is to create a favorable selling *Relationship* while seeking clues as to the nature and cause of the antipathy. Although a prospect who harbors adverse attitudes may resist the development of a favorable selling *Relationship*, resistance can often be overcome.

Example: Bucking a Bad "Inheritance"

Nina Torres sells the services of the Flying Carpet Travel Agency to businesses whose employees have substantial travel requirements. She has been trying for a long time to break through with Mike Phelps, manager of the travel section of Eureka Petroleum, but she has been getting nowhere. Today, however, she has persuaded him to have lunch with her, so she can explain her company's new computerized reservation system.

The luncheon has gone well. Mike wanted to learn about the advanced reservation system and has been impressed. Now, as he finishes his coffee, he turns to Nina and smiles.

"I'm going to tell you why I've been giving you a rough time," he announces. "Four years ago the fellow that had your job pulled a really nasty trick. Our chairman had to fly in a big hurry to Bahrein, and it was just before Christmas. You'd know how many Arab kids fly home at that time from their American schools and colleges.

"Well, practically all those Arabs fly first-class, of course, and there's just so much space. We were giving Flying Carpet a lot of business then;

but your predecessor went home early that day and swore he didn't get the word till the day after—which was too late. That put the blame on me. Our chairman flew to Bahrein tourist class—and with three stops en route! Believe me, I heard plenty about that. So I made up my mind Flying Carpet was through. And they were.

"But that guy is gone and you're here, and I figure you wouldn't do a thing like that. So we'll try your new computerized reservation system and see how it goes."

Nina had built up her selling *Relationship* with Mike to the point where he was able to shed his aversion to Flying Carpet. He put his resentment where it belonged—on the person who was no longer there, and he stopped penalizing Nina for something she didn't even know about.

But often the reason for an unfavorable attitude is known, and there is usually something you can do to overcome it. This usually requires you to convince the prospect that the offensive factor—whatever it was—will not happen again; and the better the selling *Relationship*, the more likely you are to achieve this.

Example: Overcoming a Serious Failure

Hank Berenson covers a large territory for Mogul Tubing. He used to sell a lot of tubing to Venture Plumbing Supplies, but no more.

Garth Benton, who purchases for Venture, had called Hank on a Wednesday.

"Hank, I can give you a pretty big order if you can get it to a site in Murchport Friday afternoon. This is urgent. Murchport Refrigeration is a big operation. They've had some damage, and it has to be repaired in a hurry. Rossiter Contracting has the job, and they're scheduled to complete it over the weekend. They'll shut down the refrigeration where they have to work and shift the perishables so they won't spoil. They'll be working all kinds of overtime; so you can see the urgency."

Garth then gave details of the order, and Hank checked the Mogul warehouse and found that everything needed was in inventory. He called Garth back.

"We've started loading the truck. Stop worrying."

On the way to Murchport the truck driver stopped off for supper, and he had one beer too many. The truck was in a ditch, and the driver was in a local jail. Everybody caught "flak" and Venture stopped buying from Mogul.

Hank stayed away for several months, and then one day, he showed up. Garth's receptionist announced him, and Garth came out of his office.

"I ought to punch you in the nose!" he told Hank.

"I wasn't driving that truck, Garth, and you know it," Hank replied. "I did my job. Everything you wanted was loaded—I checked that personally. And the truck should have arrived with hours to spare—I laid out the route and timed it myself. It was our newest and best truck—I checked that out also. We never had any trouble with that driver before. It was just one of those things that nobody can foresee."

"I laid it in your lap, and you messed up," Garth said.

"Just tell me one thing, Garth, one thing that I should have done and didn't."

Garth considered for a moment, and then said: "To me, you are Mogul. I know you, and when I had to take all that heat—and it was plenty hot—I naturally blamed you. But I guess you're right. I believe you did all you could to make good on your promise."

"So maybe you won't hold all that against me now, Garth?" Hank said.

"Not now, Hank. Not now. I'm glad you came by." Garth held out his hand to Hank.

Not every prospect is as honest or as level-headed as Garth Benton, and few prospects suffer so grievously from a vendor's failure to deliver on schedule. However, this example illustrates the value of an excellent selling *Relationship*. If Garth did not have the recollection of this to fall back on, Hank would not have been given another chance.

Sometimes, however, the salesperson does not have the advantage of a favorable selling *Relationship* and has no idea why he failed to close a sale. When this happens, the best course is to meet the situation frankly, head on.

Example: Overcoming the Past

Luther Jamison sells major appliances for a major manufacturer. He has made a substantial sales proposal to Roger Fenimore, buyer for a chain of appliance stores. Luther knows that his proposal "beats" the competition. But he cannot get Fenimore to buy it.

Fenimore has pointed out certain objections, and Luther has gone out of his way to meet them constructively. Because the deal would be a very good one for Fenimore's outlets, Luther cannot understand why Fenimore is holding out. Finally he decides that he must open the matter up so that the obstacle—whatever it was—can be faced.

"Mr. Fenimore," he begins, "I have made a proposal that would be very advantageous for your stores. It could be the most profitable promotion you've handled in several years. I've listened to your objections and reservations, and I've met each of them. Now, there must be some other reason why you still don't buy this promotion. Please tell me—what is the real obstacle?"

Fenimore was silent for a while. Then he spoke.

"All right, I'll tell you. The last time we did a big promotion with your company we had a very embarrassing experience. Most of our sales are on the installment plan, and we borrow on our receivables to pay our suppliers.

Well, money was tight, interest was high, and our collections were slow. We had a few other financial drains at the same time. Your company wasn't even a bit flexible. It demanded payment on schedule and made quite a fuss when we asked for a little time. Well, we managed to meet the demands, and we're a lot stronger now and our credit is very good. But there's still a lot of hard feeling around here about the way your company treated us when we were vulnerable. Maybe you'll understand now why our people don't exactly stand up and cheer at the idea of doing business with you."

Luther thought a moment before he answered.

"Thank you for telling me that, Mr. Fenimore. I didn't know about that and, of course, I had nothing to do with it. I wasn't even with the company at that time. I think I understand how you feel. I'll be glad to go over the payment provisions in my proposal to be sure they are satisfactory to you. If I have any difficulty getting approval for whatever changes you want to make, I'll tell them what you told me. In fact, I'll be glad to bring the manager of our receivables accounting here to meet you; he's a good man. The man that had that job retired about a year ago. He may have been the one that caused that difficulty. We really ought to get along well together, and your distribution is a natural for our products."

"You're right about that, young man," Fenimore replied. "If only we could count on a good working *Relationship*. So I'll take another look at your proposals, and you bring your accounting manager here next—let's see—Thursday, at three, to discuss any changes I think we should make."

Faced with a direct question, reasonably and inoffensively phrased (like Luther's), most prospects will respond (like Fenimore) if not with a full and frank disclosure of the problem, at least with some hint of its nature. And such a question also has the effect of compelling prospects to face the reasons for their attitude and, perhaps, more objectively than before.

Even when the situation involves some degree of personal antipathy to the salesperson himself, this need not prevent a sale, providing that the other conditions are favorable. If you have reason to believe that the prospect has negative feelings about you, keep the *Communication* as business-like, impersonal, and objective as possible. As in all selling, emphasize the positive values in what you are offering.

Overcoming the Prospect's Problems in Making the Purchase

Salespeople sometimes encounter situations in which the prospect has adequate positive motivation to buy and all the other Essential Conditions are met—except that there is some reason why the prospect cannot (or may not) effectuate the purchase. There may be a variety of such reasons; and there are a variety of ways in which the salesperson can surmount the obstacles to closing the sale.

There are three principal reasons why a prospect may be inhibited from finalizing a purchase which he or she definitely desires to make. These reasons are: organizational, financial, and "privileged" competition.

A: The most frequently encountered obstacles are those of organizational origin. Basically, these occur when the prospect lacks the authority (or is unwilling to take the responsibility) for committing the company to the purchase. Typically, such situations arise when:

1. The prospect's authority to commit funds for an individual purchase does not extend to the amount required to make the purchase.

2. The prospect cannot make a purchase of the nature involved without the approval, concurrence, or endorsement of other individuals (for instance, comptrollers, committees, boards, operating officials, quality assurance, research, or other technical personnel).

3. The prospect is to be the user of the purchase, but has no authority to buy.

In all such cases the salesperson has more selling to do: he or she must get to and sell whoever else must be sold, beside the original prospect. In such situations, a good selling *Relationship* with the original prospect can be especially useful in developing a positive motivation to buy in those who must participate in or make the buying decision.

B: The obstacles of financial origin are usually budgetary. For example:

1. A department of a plant, for instance—or buyer for a department in a retail operation—often has a budget (on an annual, quarterly, or monthly basis) that covers the specific purpose to which the proposed sale is related. Such allocations are often subject to tight budgetary controls.

2. Many organizations control disbursements to keep them in balance with income. This usually requires monthly adjustments and may result in the prevention of a contemplated purchase because of the (temporary) limitation of funds.
    The salesperson can react to such situations by arranging to have the purchase postponed until more funds are available; selling the idea that the advantages of an immediate purchase justify a temporary financial imbalance; or arranging to finance the purchase in such a way as to have it meet the financial requirements of the purchasing organization.

3. Some companies have policies that limit the purchase of certain classes of product or service to specifically identified suppliers. This may be based on long-term satisfactory relationship; on reciprocity

of some kind ("you buy from me, and I'll buy from you"); or on some form of organizational relationship (subsidiaries or divisions of the same corporation, etc.). Sometimes a salesperson from a competitor of a "chosen" vendor will offer a product or service that is preferable to the product or service provided by the privileged supplier but a sale is prevented by the vendor-selective purchasing policy.

Such situations call for a real "break-through," by convincing whoever controls such a policy that an exception should be made; or that the salesperson's firm should be added to the privileged list. This may not be easy to do; but the rewards can be great.

The salesperson who faces such a situation should take heart from the fact that nothing lasts forever—not even the envied position of the privileged competitor. Sooner or later the right salesperson, with the right product or service, will overcome the barrier and meet success by tempting the most exclusive prospect with irresistible benefits.

Making the Purchase Look Right

Nothing leads more surely to the closing of a sale than the prospect's feeling that "the buy looks and feels right." This means that the prospect believes that *all* the essential conditions for making a sale are met and there are no more bases for hesitation or delay.

There is a certain change of attitude in the prospect's orientation to the purchase, which straddles the transition between overcoming the negative and accepting the positive. The prospect may be thoroughly "sold" in every detail, but still somehow not ready to "sign on the dotted line." Getting the prospect over that psychological barrier—moving the prospect from the point of no more resistance to the point of "taking the step"—that is the *closing* process. It sometimes involves overcoming hesitation which no longer has a logical basis.

When this happens, be certain that all the essential conditions have, in fact, been met. Review them with the prospect, and be sure the confirmation you receive is sincere.

Some prospects are too easily led to agree to all sorts of selling arguments—but are actually unconvinced by them. Such a prospect may lead a salesperson to believe that all essential conditions have been adequately met, and the prospect is ready to buy. Yet the prospect may have reservations about and non-acceptances of the salesperson's presentation, and is in no way ready to conclude a purchase. (Some weak prospects do go ahead and buy, acting under the salesperson's selling pressure. Such sales are often canceled, soon after—perhaps by the prospect's boss or spouse.)

Make sure your prospect is indeed sold—not merely pretending to be.

Go over any element of your selling procedure that you may have any reason to believe has left any vestige of doubt or resistance. Once you have checked the situation out, and *know* that the prospect is thoroughly sold in principle, then the time has come to close in fact.

One of the most effective tactics for "making the buy look right" is to get the prospect to think about the actual realization of the anticipated *Benefits*, following the purchase.

Example: Reviewing the Benefits

Oscar Moss has almost sold a big woodburning furnace to Reginald Semple, a wealthy horsebreeder. That is, Semple has been thoroughly sold, but is hesitating to sign the contract, which includes the cost of installation in Semple's large home on his stud farm. Oscar knows how to provide the psychological nudge that will put Semple's signature on the dotted line.

"I'm a little curious, Mr. Semple," Oscar says. "We don't often install woodburning furnaces this large, and I am wondering about the size of the dollar savings you anticipate. When we hook it up to your oil burner, as you know, it can provide all the heat you need to keep your thermostats from starting your oil burner. Now, how much oil did you burn last winter?"

"I told you I have a big house—eighteen rooms. But it's not very well insulated. I believe we averaged about 4000 gallons of fuel oil each winter over the past couple of years."

"You ought to save most of that. Now, have you any idea what it will cost you for the wood?"

"The wood? It won't cost me anything! That is, it'll be cut on my own land. I have at least 100 acres of woods. It'll be cut by my farm workers, when they aren't busy in the fields and stables. I'll have to buy a few chain saws, and pay for some extra gas, and that's about it."

"Well, then, Mr. Semple! Are you telling me you expect this furnace to save you maybe $5000 a year? That's terrific! You'll practically have a free ride after the first year."

"That's about right, I guess. Say—how soon can you get it installed?"

By getting Semple to re-think—himself—the actual benefits he expected to enjoy as a result of the purchase, Oscar has, in effect, caused Semple to "sell himself all over again." When the prospect develops his or her own perception of the expected benefits—in terms of his or her own circumstances, plans, and values—it has a far stronger psychological effect than when even the most skilled salesperson tries to do it for him or her. The prospect thus generates his or her own Positive Motivation to buy, using all the ideas the salesperson has presented that fit the prospect's own perceptions.

This kind of final "kicker" can overcome most cases of last-minute hesitation.

How to Avoid Being "Put Off"

The most usual form of "hold-out," after a prospect has acknowledged satisfaction in all the essential conditions, is in delay. The prospect wants to put off the final commitment.

Sometimes the prospect wants "to be sure," "to think about it," or "to sleep on it." This attitude is often due to the novelty of the experience of making such a decision; the prospect needs to "get used to the idea."

Some prospects also lack confidence and fear they may be making a mistake—or that others will think this. Or, the prospect may have a conflicting perception of the purchase: "Yes, it's well worth that price, but it's a lot of money to spend."

In all such situations it is important to determine whether or not there is some special, objective reason for delay, or whether it is simply the inability of the prospect to take action implementing a virtual decision to buy. If the first condition obtains, then it may well be necessary for that reason—whatever it is—to be taken care of or satisfied. Otherwise it becomes a matter of overcoming the prospect's procrastination.

People differ greatly in character and temperament, of course; some people have difficulty in making and acting on decisions (while others make them and act on them too readily without due consideration). It is also true that people are more likely to act on a decision about matters with which they are familiar, and about which they can therefore feel some degree of confidence; while the same people may behave quite differently about matters with which they have had little experience. In situations where the prospect's hesitation is due to such natural factors, it often helps for the salesperson to review the considerations that have won apparent acceptance. Going over arguments that have already been effective—with added emphasis and with the reinforcing power of summarization— can "accentuate the positive" and overcome residual doubts, so that the prospect feels comfortable in finalizing the transaction.

The most often used techniques for closing a sale are

1. making it seem natural and easy to formalize the purchase;
2. getting the prospect used to the idea of commitment to buy;
3. leading the prospect to accept the act of buying as part of a logical series of correct personal decisions that have already been made.

However, many individuals seem unable to bring themselves to enter into the closing without some kind of "help" which the salesperson must provide. This usually requires a confident, positive attitude on the part of the salesperson, which indicates that the time to close has arrived. And this kind of attitude can usually be demonstrated by a simple question.

The classical tactic is for the salesperson to ask a question that *assumes* the sale is made and requires an answer to some detail of preference among alternatives. For example:

"Shall I send it or will you take it with you?"

"Will you pay cash or charge it?"

"What day do you want it delivered?"

"Do you want these packaged in dozens or hundreds?"

"Will you have the black or the red?"

"Should we ship it by rail or truck?"

The prospect's choice of one of the alternatives is equivalent to a definite decision to buy and should be followed up with the appropriate formality—the contractual agreement.

Sometimes prospects "waffle." They appear to be unable to "stay sold." They give every indication of having made a buying decision—and even say so—but they draw back before making a formal commitment. Such individuals often need a bit of "help" in the form of a "push" by the salesperson. This is not to advocate "bulldozing" the weak prospect—a process that may verge upon or actually involve the unethical. What is meant here is a psychological "boost" to help the prospect do what he or she has really decided to do, but somehow cannot bring him or herself to act out.

They are like the inexperienced swimmer who hesitates on the diving board, afraid to take the plunge.

What is needed is a friend who puts an arm around the timid diver and says something like: "Come on, now! You've already made up your mind to jump in or you wouldn't be out on this board. All you have to do is to make your body carry out the decision your mind has made."

The salesperson who has been able to develop a good selling *Relationship* can be such a friend.

How to Analyze and Overcome Sales Resistance

Sometimes a salesperson encounters what is known as "sales resistance"—an apparently negative attitude toward the selling effort; an attitude that may be characterized by a lack of receptivity of the salesperson's *Communication* ranging from skepticism to overt rebuttal; from frank unwillingness to listen to simple lack of interest. For instance:

1. What you are trying to sell provides no *Benefits* that would interest the prospect. (If this is so, then you are wasting everybody's time.)

2. There is at least one *Benefit* that would interest the prospect, but you haven't tried to sell it. (It is up to you to find out what that benefit is.)

3. The *Benefit(s)* you have been trying to sell could be of interest to the prospect, but you haven't *Communicated* with the prospect in

a way that stimulates his interest. (You'd better find out what the trouble is and get on the right "wavelength.")

4. You are selling a *Benefit* that is of potential interest to the prospect, but there is some *negative motivation* (other than *Relationship*) at work that keeps the prospect from being interested in the sale you are trying to make.

5. Your *Relationship* with the prospect keeps him from being interested. You need to understand the prospect's perception of you, why this perception constitutes an obstacle to your selling effort, and what you can do to change and to improve that perception.

Your first response to such behavior should be to re-evaluate the whole situation in terms of this primary question: Is this individual really a prospect?

The answer to this question should be carefully evaluated along the lines suggested in Chapter 3. If the answer turns out to be that the individual is not a prospect, that should explain his behavior. However, if the salesperson continues to evaluate the individual as a prospect, then the situation should be analyzed as follows:

A. What values of this prospect have been neglected or inadequately satisfied in your presentation of *Benefits*? In this connection, it may be vital to consider the effects of competition and of the attractiveness of competitive *Benefits* to the prospect's values.

1. Prospect resists; does not accept salesperson's presentation of *Benefits*. Prospect's resistant attitude toward salesperson's offering and toward salesperson is made up of many elements; based on prospect's needs and wants, interests, values, and perceptions affected by different elements in salesperson's *Communication*.

2. Salesperson's *Communication* is made up of many elements. Some are not relevant to prospect's values, and some are not appropriately communicated.

3. Some of prospect's perceptions are favorable (P1), but others are not (P2). Feedback from prospect can tell salesperson what to emphasize (and what to "drop").

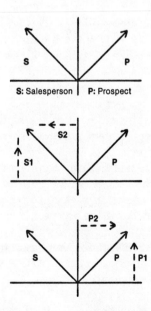

4. Feedback reveals that prospect's adverse perceptions (P3) are opposed to elements of salesperson's presentation.

5. Feedback reveals that salesperson should eliminate, modify, or de-emphasize element S2 and further develop and emphasize S1, which prospect accepts. P1 leads to Positive Motivation to Buy.

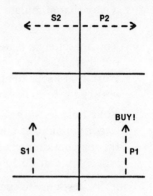

How to Adapt Communication to Prospect's Values

B. If all the *Benefits* relating to the values of the prospect have been presented, we may ask whether there has been a failure in *Communication*. Has the *Communication* been appropriate? Understood? Misunderstood?

C. If the prospect's sales resistance cannot be accounted for by careful consideration of A and B, we may ask whether there is a problem in the *Relationship* that can account for the resistant attitude or, could it be due to some factor in the competitive situation?

Another important kind of sales resistance is based on a lack of interest, which may be due to the prospect's unfamiliarity with the product or service being offered. This lack of interest often parallels a prospect's first or early acquaintance with a new product or service.

When introducing a new or unfamiliar product, you still must "Sell the *Benefits*" in terms of the values important to the prospect. If what you offer involves new and unfamiliar values, it may be necessary to *"educate"* the prospect to an appreciation of such values.

There may also be a kind of competition with the past: resistance to the replacement of previously satisfying products or services, as well as the basic resistance to change, and aversion to the unfamiliar.

All of this calls for identifying and addressing those more basic values which account for the positive motivation of the prospect, and which the products or services you offer can satisfy, rather than dwelling upon details unfamiliar to the prospect, which may not, in themselves, appear to be *Benefits*.

For instance, emphasize the purposes and advantages of what you offer, and do so in terms of basic values (economy, durability, reliability, ease of maintenance, etc.).

Sometimes an alert salesperson can make a selling breakthrough by finding a new market for a product. Here is an example from our past.

Example: Warming Pans in Cuba!

In colonial times people didn't have central heating, and in the long, cold winters you couldn't be warm unless you were near a fire in a stove or in a fireplace. People especially hated to have to crawl into a chilly bed. So they used warming pans in their beds. Warming pans were shallow pans made of copper or brass, usually about a foot across, with a hinged lid and a long wooden handle. People would put hot coals in these pans and then use the pans to warm up their beds on wintry nights.

These warming pans were very popular in New England, where the winters were especially harsh. The "benefits" which the warming pans provided were obvious enough not to need very skillful selling. Of course, as you went south, the benefits of the warming pan were less and less appreciated; when you got far enough south, you could expect to meet quite a lot of sales resistance. This kind of sales resistance did not arise from any objection to warming pans, but only to a lack of interest. The benefit associated with them in the cold climates had no values in a warm climate.

What would you think of the possibility of selling warming pans in the Caribbean?

Well, there used to be a character in those days in Newburyport, Massachusetts, named Timothy Dexter, who owned sailing ships and traded all over the world. He became quite well known as a super-salesman, and probably did more than any other one person to establish the reputation of the Yankee trader for ingenuity and enterprise. This Lord Timothy Dexter, as he liked to call himself, actually succeeded in selling a whole shipload of warming pans—in Cuba!

It seems that one of Lord Timothy's ships had carried a cargo of Cuban rum to England and was returning to Cuba for more rum. Rather than return empty, they took the only cargo they could get: brass warming pans. Of course, in Cuba they couldn't sell them for their original purpose.

Dexter realized that if he was to sell his warming pans, he would have to come up with a *Benefit* that would interest the Cubans—and he did! He showed them how they could use his warming pans to make sugar—by filling a pan with sugar-cane juice and holding it over a fire until the fluid boiled away. And Dexter sold the whole shipload of pans.

You may never have a problem like selling warming pans in Cuba, but whenever you run into the problem of sales resistance due to lack of interest, remember what Timothy Dexter did about selling a *Benefit* that *was* of interest to his prospects.

How to Overcome Negative Motivation

There are two kinds of sales resistance. One kind is due to a lack of interest in the *Benefits*. The other kind arises from negative motivation.

The first kind of sales resistance may be overcome by determining which of the potential *Benefits* can stimulate positive motivation and emphasizing these in the most appropriate way. But negative motivation is something else again. It means that some of the prospect's values are working against you, so that some kind of adverse perception must be overcome before you can even get to a neutral, "lack of interest" level of zero motivation.

Negative motivation, of course, can easily kill a sale—and sometimes it doesn't take very much of a negative to do just that. Some negatives are very hard to overcome.

Negative motivation comes from two sources. One of these pre-exists in the prospect: it consists of values, needs, knowledge, ideas, impressions, beliefs, preferences, tastes, and all the other elements of the individual's psychological make-up that can affect attitudes, behavior, and buying decisions.

The other source of negative motivation is the salesperson—the prospect may react negatively to something he or she says or does; or the way he or she says it or does it; or to the personality of the salesperson.

The prospect may already have developed a negative evaluation of what you are offering, before the prospect ever saw or heard of you. In such situations you only have the problem of overcoming that, on an impersonal, objective basis.

Basically, such situations call for re-examination of the values important to the prospect and ensuring that all the relevant *Benefits* you can offer are *Communicated* as effectively as possible. If the negative reaction is about something you have said, you have the additional problem of realizing what it was that caused the reaction and understanding why, so you can work at overcoming it.

As with illness, it is far better to prevent negative motivation than it is to let it happen and then have to try to "cure" it. The best way to avoid negative motivation is to understand the prospect and the particular values he associates with the product, your company, or you. If you listen carefully, you should be able to learn what subjects or ideas to avoid; or, if they cannot be avoided, at least how to handle them so as to cause the least negative reaction.

If the negative reaction is against yourself or something you have said, it is essential to avoid anything that could possibly reinforce that reaction. Be objective and impersonal and present each point you make with convincing third-party reference, support, or proof. This should help to separate your selling effort from yourself, as a person, in the perception of the prospect.

Remember that negative motivations based on inadequate or inaccurate information *can* be overcome, and that when they are overcome, there is likely to be a favorable reaction toward you. When the prospect realizes that whatever was holding him back was based on misapprehension, he should be "ripe" for a successful closing.

How to Overcome Competition:
The Three Basic Strategies

There are many different things you can do to overcome competition, but basically—strategically—there are just three ways. All the tactics you can possibly apply can activate only one or more of these three basic strategies. The three essential elements of Motivational Selling Leverage implement these three basic strategies. So let us analyze the problems of overcoming competition in terms of those three essentials.

Relations. A buying decision may be based upon salesperson-prospect *Relationship*. The *Relationship* may derive wholly or partly from organizational rather than personal considerations, and may affect the final result directly or indirectly.

To overcome competitive advantage in salesperson-prospect relationships, it is necessary to:

1. Work to improve your *Relationship* with the prospect by eliminating or reducing the basis for negative reactions; enhancing credibility and acceptance of your *Communication* to the prospect; and providing information that can help you understand the basis for your competitive disadvantage.

2. Re-evaluate the prospect's value-orientation toward the prospective purchase and re-examine the attractiveness of your *Benefits* as compared with those of your competitor. Develop the comparison *in terms of values perceived by the prospect.*

3. Re-design your *Communication* to provide maximum effectiveness in emphasizing any and all advantages over the competition which you can offer, in terms of the comparison made in 2 (above).

Benefits. A buying decision is based on the prospect's perception of the comparative balance of *Benefits*. This is the way a prospect usually arrives at a buying decision, but he or she may not be fully informed or may not be using good judgment.

To overcome a competitive advantage in prospect perception of comparative *Benefits*, it is necessary to determine the values influencing the situation; and the actualities of the *Benefits* involved, and of their prospective application by the prospect or the prospect's organization or principal.

1. Determine if the *Benefits* are inherent (characteristics of the product or service itself) or ancillary (price, financing, delivery, packaging, etc.).

2. Determine if the product or service can be modified to provide *Benefits* which the prospect will evaluate as equal or superior to those offered competitively.

3. Determine if the ancillary Benefits can be modified to provide *Benefits* which the prospect will evaluate as equal or superior to those offered competitively.

4. Determine if you can offer one or some *Benefits* in enhanced form to outweigh the advantage held by the competition. This could take any form attractive to the prospect.

5. Determine if the prospect has complete understanding of the values involved and of the ways in which the competitive *Benefits* relate to these. If there is inadequacy of understanding, it may be feasible to "educate" the prospect or to carry the selling effort to another level (i.e., from purchasing agent to operating executive, from wife to husband, etc.).

Communication. A buying decision may be based on a prospect's inadequate understanding of the competitive situation. This may result from failure of a salesperson to *Communicate* effectively with the prospect. It may also result from unjustifiable claims or representations by a competitor.

To overcome a competitor advantage, it is necessary to review and evaluate the *Communication* process to ensure that every positive factor has been appropriately presented and emphasized and to identify any negative factor that may require rebuttal.

1. Review the values significant to the prospect.

2. Review the ways in which the *Benefits* have been *Communicated* in terms of these values.

3. Note any omissions, discrepancies, or deficiencies in *Communicating* the *Benefits* to the prospect.

4. Recall any questions, comments, etc., by the prospect that may be symptomatic of failure to understand, misapprehension, prejudice, or adverse reaction.

5. Consider realistically the *Benefits* offered by the competition in relation to the values significant to the prospect. Evaluate the effects of this competitive situation on the matters under 2, 3, and 4.

6. Develop a list of supplementary items to be *Communicated* to the prospect to emphasize positive factors and to overcome negative factors recognized in 5.

Example: Beating the Competition

Joshua Lell has a regional agency for a sprinkler system—the kind that pops up out of the ground when it is turned on. He has a fairly standard sales pitch that he uses effectively with homeowners. Now Josh is trying to make a sale to a 40-acre, private golf club, but he seems to be losing out to a competitor who specializes in sprinkler systems for golf courses and parks.

Josh has telephoned the sales manager of the company he represents to ask for advice.

"You are in a new ball game," Josh is told. "When you sell our system to a homeowner, you stress convenience. But with big installations the benefits are very different. Then, you are selling the labor-saving angle—which should amortize the cost in three to five years. To make this a competitive point, you have to stress the low maintenance requirements, high durability, easy replacement of sprinkler heads, etc. We're sending you technical data on the superiority of our system for golf courses."

Josh learned fast. He began by cultivating the grounds-keeper of the golf club and the members of the Greens Committee. Based on what they told him and using the product information he received, he analyzed the values important to his prospect and emphasized the *Benefits* he could offer to satisfy those values. When he made his presentation to the Greens Committee of the golf club, it was very different from his usual pitch to homeowners.

"Now you're talking our language," the chairman of the committee told him. "Those are the points that are important to us."

Josh made the sale, and he did it by following the three basic strategies: *Relations*, *Benefits*, and *Communication*.

There Is a Way to Sell Almost Any Prospect

Make up your mind that:

1. There *is* a way to sell almost *any* prospect.
2. The best way to sell one prospect is different from the best way to sell another prospect.
3. The only way to know that best way for each prospect is to find it out—perhaps from the prospect him- or herself.
4. The prospect will tell you that only (or give you the chance to find out) if he or she wants to, and he or she will want to if he or she needs what you sell or if he or she is inclined in that direction by your *Relationship* with him or her.

In the following examples, notice the difference in the approach of Ed Kurtz and Nat Sloper.

Example: The Stone Wall

Ed Kurtz sells machine tools for the International Equipment Corporation. He is calling on the purchasing agent of Perfect Castings, Inc., Kent Byles.

ED: Mr. Byles, I'm sure your engineering staff knows about our new Multishaper and what it can do in your semi-finishing department.

BYLES: Yes, I'm sure they do.

ED: I'd be glad to run a demonstration on your own blanks—

BYLES: That won't be necessary.

ED: But we would like to be considered when you are in the market—

BYLES: Every qualified supplier will be considered when the time comes, and that time isn't now. Anything else?

Ed leaves, frustrated. Perfect Castings does not seem to be a prospect.

Example: The Open Door

Nat Sloper sells machine tools for Productivity Machine Company. He is calling on the same purchasing agent, Kent Byles.

NAT: How's your wife, Kent?

BYLES: Meg's fine—she's studying for her doctorate.

NAT: My wife Jane is thinking of going back to school, too. Now that the kids are older, she has more time. How about the youngsters?

BYLES: OK, I guess. Joe is doing very well in school, and Nellie played a piano solo at the PTA a couple of weeks ago.

NAT: That's great. And how's your golf?

BYLES: Rusty.

NAT: We'll have to try it out next time I'm in town. What else is new?

BYLES: Well, nothing at the moment. But you might be interested in knowing that we're going to bid on a big contract for Jepson Engine Works. If it comes through we'll have to tool up for it, and two or three of your models might qualify—but they'd probably have to be modified.

NAT: That certainly does interest me, Kent, and I appreciate your telling me. How soon can I find out about the details?

BYLES: You'll have to get that from engineering—they haven't given it to me, yet. Hold on a minute while I call Lem Sholes. If he's in and free, he could give you what they have on it so far.

NAT: Great. I'd love to talk to Lem.

If Perfect Castings decides to buy the machines, engineering will give the specifications to Kent Byles, and he will pass them on to all eligible suppliers, including Ed Kurtz' International Equipment Corporation. Only Nat Sloper will be ready.

The two examples above reveal two very different selling situations. It would appear that Ed Kurtz' problem, Kent Byles, is a very different kind of person from Nat Sloper's Kent Byles—but they are both the same Kent Byles. Unless there are factors in the situation that compel Byles to treat Ed and Nat differently, the difference between Ed Kurtz' Kent Byles and Nat Sloper's Kent Byles is due to the difference between Ed Kurtz and Nat Sloper. Prospects (and nonprospects) are human—just as human as salespersons; they react to other humans in the ways that are natural to them. Prospects differ—just as salespersons differ; they react differently to salespersons and even to the same salesperson. Since it is ultimately the prospect who makes the buying decision, it is up to the salesperson to do an effective job of selling. This usually requires adaptation of the selling process to the prospect. The three primary areas for effective adaptation are, of course, the three elements of Motivational Selling Leverage: the nature of the *Relationship*, the matching of *Benefits* to prospect values, and the effectiveness of *Communication*.

The salesperson who understands and accepts these principles, and who has learned how to apply them (as outlined in this book) with adequate *product knowledge* ought to be able to close a sale with *any* prospect (a true prospect—one who would evaluate seriously the desirability of making a favorable buying decision). Confidence and determination also help.

Here is an example of success in closing a sale which many would have considered impossible. Read it, and remember that there have been many such triumphs of salespersonship under the most unpromising of circumstances—when the basic principles that govern all such transactions were truly understood and capably acted upon.

Example: Don't Let Unfavorable Conditions Stop You: How Jane Morgan Made a "Hopeless" Sale

Jane Morgan owns a pest control service, Total Extermination, Inc. It competes on a local basis—especially for the larger contracts—with much bigger national and regional firms.

There is a resort area a couple of hundred miles away from the city where Jane's service generally operates. One organization, the Pleasant Recreation Corporation, owns and operates most of the hotels, restaurants, and other facilities there. Their pest control contract is a big one. It is signed annually on the basis of competitive bidding by large pest control organizations. One year Jane decided to go after it.

First she discussed the matter with a friend, Herb Nettles, who had a job managing one of the restaurants for Pleasant Recreation, and knew their operations pretty well.

"Jane—dear Jane," Herb began, "it's hopeless! You haven't a prayer. Everything is against you. First of all, you aren't big enough to handle it. You'd need more people, more equipment, more trucks, more supervision than you put on all your other jobs together. You have no experience on big jobs like that. You'd be bidding against the biggest and best firms in the business—if they'd even let you bid. I doubt if they would consider you qualified. That's all handled by their manager of operations, old Archie Slinger— and I have to tell you, he's a tough old geezer to deal with. On top of that, he doesn't think women should be in business."

Jane found that everything Herb told her was true. She couldn't even make an appointment to go over and see old Slinger; his secretary told her, on the phone, they just didn't have her on the list of eligible bidders. She found out that the firm currently holding the contract that she wanted had set up a local facility to handle the job; she had no advantage there. She had no *Relationship* with Pleasant Recreation at all; they weren't interested in any *Benefits* she could offer; so far she hadn't even *Communicated* with them!

But that didn't stop her. She wrote to their legal office (not operations) and asked for a blank copy of the contract—and got it. She studied it very carefully; then spent a week (as an ordinary paying guest) at the resort. But instead of enjoying the facilities, she used the time and proximity to study the situation in detail; even discussing the insect and rodent problems, and how they were being handled, with as many knowledgeable people as she could reach on an informal basis.

Then she spent a great deal of time and care writing up a proposal. She went into a lot of detail about exactly what she would do; and where and how she would do it; and why it would be more advantageous than the present service. She also accompanied her proposal with a covering letter, listing and describing her experience in terms of individual problems, solutions, and successes. This was in order to emphasize the *quality* of her service, since she couldn't speak of volume. Finally, she urged that, if she could not have the whole contract, they should consider splitting it. Jane proposed that they give her a separate contract, on a trial basis, to see what could be done with certain areas that presented special problems—these involving the treatment of certain sites especially attractive to pests, and those presenting certain difficulties in taking effective countermeasures. But she also stressed minimizing inconvenience and offensiveness to guests caused by some necessary procedures, such as fumigation, odor-emitting chemicals, baits attractive to pets, etc.

Well, in due course she got a call from Slinger's secretary Jane drove over to see Slinger. He was coldly businesslike, but reasonable. He asked her about some of the ideas in her proposal, commenting that no one else had raised some of those points. He nodded when he heard her answers; they ended up negotiating a deal that was pretty much like the one she had suggested.

Jane had overcome what seemed to be totally unfavorable conditions. She did it by carefully working out attractive *Benefits*, *Communicating* them in a way that was effective, and thereby creating enough of a *Relationship* to make the sale.

Now, "go thou and do likewise!"

★ ★ ── Index ────────────────── ★ ★